Play On, Christina Nott

Ed Adams

a firstelement production

Ed Adams

First published in Great Britain in 2020 by firstelement
Copyright © 2020 Ed Adams
Directed by thesixtwenty

10 9 8 7 6 5 4 3 2 1
All rights reserved.

No part of this publication may be reproduced, stored in a retrieval system, or transmitted, in any form or by any means, without the prior permission in writing of the publisher, nor be otherwise circulated in any form or binding or cover other than that in which it is published and without a similar condition including this condition being imposed on the subsequent purchaser.

Every effort has been made to acknowledge the appropriate copyright holders. The publisher regrets any oversight and will be pleased to rectify any omission in future editions.

Similarities with real people or events is unintended and coincidental.

A CIP catalogue record for this book is available from the British Library.

ISBN 13 : 978-1-913818-06-7

eBook ISBN : 978-1-913818-07-4

Printed and bound in Great Britain by Ingram Spark

rashbre
an imprint of firstelement.co.uk
rashbre@mac.com

http://www.ed-adam.net

Play On, Christina Nott

Ed Adams

To the band

Thanks

A big thank you for the tolerance and bemused support from all of those around me. To those who know when it is time to say, " step away from the keyboard!" and to those who don't.

To Julie for that kind of understanding that only comes with really knowing me.

To thesixtwenty.co.uk for direction.

To the NaNoWriMo gang for the continued inspiration and encouragement.

To John, for many hours of intense scrutiny. To Steve for his encouragement and that original Indian restaurant meal in Staines. To Georgina for cover ideas.

And, of course, thanks to the extensive support via the random scribbles of rashbre via http://rashbre2.blogspot.com and its cast of amazing and varied readers whether human, twittery, smoky, cool kats, photographic, dramatic, musical, anagrammed, globalized or simply maxed-out.

Not forgetting the cast of characters involved in producing this; they all have virtual lives of their own.

And of course, to you, dear reader, for at least 'giving it a go'.

Books by Ed Adams include:

Triangle Trilogy		About
1	The Triangle	Dirty money? Here's how to clean it
2	The Square	Weapons of Mass Destruction – don't let them get on your nerves
3	The Circle	The desert is no place to get lost
4	The Ox Stunner	The Triangle Trilogy – thick enough to stun an ox
		(all feature Jake, Bigsy, Clare, Chuck Manners)
Archangel Collection		
1	Archangel	Sometimes I am necessary
2	Raven	An eye that sees all between darkness and light
3	Card Game	Throwing oil on a troubled market
4	Magazine Clip	the above three in one heavy book.
5	Play On, Christina Nott	Christina Nott, on Tour for the FSB
		(all feature Jake, Bigsy, Clare, Chuck Manners)
Stand-Alone Novels		
1	Coin	Get rich quick with Cybercash – just don't tell GCHQ
2	Pulse	Want more? Just stay away from the edge
3	Edge	Power can't be left to trust
4	Now the Science	the above three in one heavy book.

About Ed Adams Novels:

Triangle Trilogy		About
1	Triangle	Money laundering within an international setting.
2	Square	A viral nerve agent being shipped by terrorists and WMDs
3	Circle	In the Arizona deserts, with the Navajo; about missiles stolen from storage.
4	Ox Stunner	the above three in one heavy book.
		(all feature Jake, Bigsy, Clare, Chuck Manners)
Archangel Collection		
1	Archangel	Biographical adventures of Russian trained Archangel, who, as Christina Nott, threads her way through other Triangle novels.
2	Raven	Big business gone bad and being a freemason won't absolve you
3	Card Game	Raven Pt 2 – Russian oligarchs attempt to take control
4	Magazine Clip	the above three in one heavy book.
5	Play On, Christina Nott	Christina Nott, on Tour for the FSB
		(all feature Jake, Bigsy, Clare, Chuck Manners)
Stand-Alone Novels		
1	Coin	cyber cash manipulation by the Russian state.
2	Pulse	Sci-Fi dystopian blood management with nano-bots
3	Edge	World end climate collapse and sham discovered during magnetite mining from Jupiter's moon Ganymede
4	Now the Science	the above three in one heavy book.

TABLE OF CONTENTS

Thanks 1
Books by Ed Adams include:.. 2
About Ed Adams Novels:.. 3

PART ONE 8

Saint Petersburg 9
Drop the Mike 10
Nevsky Prospekt.. 12
Bellevue Hotel, Dresden.. 18
Deep Cover 21
Hydra headed 24
Backwater 27

The Mission 30
Dead men tell no tales 31
Purloined in Petrograd 38

About a band.. 43
Talking about... Pop Music. 44
Shrike 47
Meet the Band 52
Rehearsal... 59
Commode.. 61

About the Money 63
How it started 64
Graduates.. 70
Whistle Blower 77

About a Tour 82
Clare 83

Rehearsal 2	85
What we'll do on the road	94

Spencer **96**
- Meet the Russians 97
- Pavle Darchidze 102
- Bakir Jamalov 114
- Oliver Trask 121
- Funnel 128
- Yaroslav Valerijovych Petruk 130
- Plan 135

The Heist **140**
- Saint Petersburg in clear 141
- Rehearsal 3 153
- Putin's casino 159

PART TWO 162

Trigger **163**
- Friday flyway 164
- Business Class 167
- Putin's dacha 175

Follow Me **185**
- Follow the Money 186
- Frankfurt Flughafen 189
- Layover 193

Big in Japan **195**
- Tokyo 196
- Erebus 199
- Stadium Rock 203
- Showtime 212
- Heavysick ZERO 220

Austin Rules	223
Yakuza	225
Saito Eiji	230

Hardboiled ... 237
Debrief	238
Tokyo Andez Hotel	240
Spanner	244
Identified	245
Galactix	250
Dreamliner	252

Los Angeles ... 253
LAX	254
Thursday morning	256
Thursday Evening	259
What happened in Sydney?	267
LA Music Weekly	271
Rodeo Drive	275

PART THREE ... 279

Seattle ... 280
Seattle	281
Smells like Teen Spirit	290
Stella shakes Seattle - my blog.	291
This room ain't big enough for the both of us	294
Seattle Space Needle	297
New York, New York	306
MOMA Nights	310
Fulton Street	318
Deutsch Union Bank	320
Pier 17	327

EMP ... 336

Back in Seattle	337
EMP Sky Church	340
The Manhattanite - Music News	342
BBC America News	346
Fairmont, breakfast buffet.	347

Triples all round **348**
   Setup Spencer 349
   Miami 1000 Tower 354
   Seattle Fairmont 362

Ed Adams

PART ONE

Saint Petersburg

"It was a marvellous night, the sort of night one only experiences when one is young.

The sky was so bright, and there were so many stars that, gazing upward, one couldn't help wondering how so many whimsical, wicked people could live under such a sky."

'White Nights and Other Stories'.

Fyodor Dostoevsky

Drop the Mike

"I'm going to Russia," said Christina.

Across the street, someone was listening in. He had arranged a shotgun microphone and a reflector and was picking up the sound across free air. It had that phase shift reminiscent of old radios.

"Yes, I've been called back," Christina added, "I knew that once I'd contacted the FSB, my name would rise right to the top of their lists... What is the saying? 'Out of sight out of mind' ."

"How long?" asked Clare.

"Don't worry, you guys will be the first to know. They have some kind of mission set up for me. They said it involves some travel. And you know what? They want me to be Christina Nott."

"In that case, you'll need your manager!" said Clare.

"Let's let it run for a while, I need to find out what I'm supposed to do first," replied Christina.

The audio seemed to go into a tunnel at this point. The guy with the reflector microphone could see that Christina was moving about in the office.

"Where are you..." The sound trailed off.

"Sss. Pppp. Gggg," answered Christina.

"I've lost it," said the man with the microphone. He sat in front of a small mixer desk and an array of wires.

"Keep trying," said the severe-looking woman sitting in the room. She looked back towards her laptop screen.

Nevsky Prospekt

Snow in St Petersburg. An icy wind blows in from the sea. In the cafe, Irina Morozova was sitting across the table from Christina Nott, now using the name Alya Sokolova.

"This was Putin's city once," said Irina Morozova.

"I heard, we were told about it in Arkhangelsk," answered Christina. She eyed Irina carefully; a young-looking mid-40s, dark shoulder length hair, slimly built and very toned, she had worn a leather jacket on the way into the cafe but had now thrown it across the back of the chair. Christina observed the way she moved, like an athlete. Christina couldn't help herself from thinking that she'd need a weapon to take her down.

"Ah yes, Alya Sokolova, the Archangel, so many names 'Christina Nott'," replied Irina, "Does it seem strange to be asked to work with someone like me?"

"Not at all," answered Alya, "I've always been waiting for a chance to work with one of the people who have seen the fall and rise of the Motherland,"

"Careful with that talk," smiled Irina, "You never know who is listening."

"What still?" asked, Alya.

"They probably still have the original wires and microphones set up in here," said Irina, "Just like the old days."

"You know, I was here once before, a long time ago, " said Alya, "It has hardly changed though - it is more like a museum."

They were sitting in Literaturnoye Kafe, the historical cafe once frequented by Alexander Pushkin, Nikolai Gogol and Fyodor Dostoyevsky. A musician was playing earnest Russian tunes on a grand piano.

"For this time, I told the FSB I wanted to revive my cover story - a musician - and they sent me here to St Petersburg. It's a little strange. I knew if I called Blackbird then he would ask me for something in return."

"Yes, Blackbird briefed me, Colonel Sokolova. You are expected to meet me here and then to accompany me on my tour around the world, literally riding shotgun."

They both smiled.

"Good blinis," observed Alya, "with the salmon."

"Yes - don't order lemonade or water here though," said Irina.

"Why's that?"

"Well, Pushkin asked for lemonade before his fatal duel, and Tchaikovsky caught cholera from the tap water, or so the stories go," answered Irina.

"That mannequin, it's supposed to be Pushkin writing a poem?" asked Alya, gesturing towards the window.

"Yes - for the tourists," explained Irina.

"So what's our story?" asked Alya, "And do I get to be Christina again?"

"Yes, you do," answered Irina, "I'm to be your A&R representative. There's another guy named Eckhart Bloch who is to be your publicist. Of course, they are both fronts and neither of us has any deep knowledge of the music industry. It means we can be seen around with you and your tour which is the front for our FSB business."

Alya was surprised by this development. "I'm getting two FSB agents to help me restart my music career?" she asked, somewhat incredulously.

"Well, that and the other mission. If you don't mind I'll keep that to myself for the moment. All the elements link to one objective, though. It means we can run various situations; that's one in Japan and a couple in the United States. We'll be heading for Tokyo and then on to LA. You - Christina - provide perfect cover."

"So why do I start here in Saint Petersburg?" asked Alya.

"Mainly because it's where both myself and Eckhart live," answered Irina.

"So, you've been here since when Putin was running the place?" asked Alya.

"That's right, St Petersburg and I have a long history. I was first here when the Soviet Union ceased to exist. It was a free-for-all. Everywhere you looked you could see people attempting to sell anything, everything, literally from the street. Even gasoline, in polythene canisters. There were an older generation here who could still remember the city from wartime; the Second World War - the blockade of the city."

"I was here once, but in those days it was very messy times," said Alya.

Irina continued, "Then there was the hyperinflation. Some money men had issued currency which could buy roubles. The other currency cost the same, but one unit could buy ten roubles. It was a crooked farce."

"How did you first meet Putin?"

"It took a while, but I became assigned to his security detail," answered Irina, "When Putin first appeared, no-one around here knew much about him. He had been based in Dresden. I think he was thirty-nine when he became mayor of the city.

"He arrived and knew how to create his own back-story. He hired a documentary-maker to cast him in a positive light - to humanise him. That filmmaker, Igor Shadkhan was a Jew and had made films on the horrors of the Soviet Gulags. But Shadkhan was a person who had always criticised the Soviet authorities.

"Somehow he was taken in by Putin - some might say he was recruited. They became friends and Putin seemed to persuade him that he was a real progressive and not part of the old guard. So, we get a film where Putin can stress the wonderful qualities of the KGB."

Alya nodded, "I remember Putin made schools study Aleksandr Solzhenitsyn, from around 2009. The Gulag Archipelago became a required reading. I remember reading about zeks - the "*zakliuchennyi*" (prisoners) through the Gulag, starting with their arrest, the show trials, then initial internment; transport to the "archipelago"; the use of the slave labour gangs and even the practice of internal exile after the original prison sentence,"

" Yes, well, if Shadkhan didn't pull punches on that Gulag documentary, he did on the one about Putin.

"He painted over the cracks and Putin describes many acts as 'betrayals of the Motherland', to be punished with the full force of the law. Bribes and corruption, he said, had no place with the modern officials. And as for being an 'official', a *chinovnik*, the word need not have any negative connotation, he claimed.

"He'd served his country as a military *chinovnik*; now he was a civilian official, serving – as he had before – his country 'outside the realm of political competition'.

Alya grimaced, "It sounds like an object lesson in propaganda - The way that Putin chose Shadkhan to make the film to show the world that he had served as an officer in the feared and hated KGB. "

Irina continued, "He knew what he was doing. Admitting links to the KGB could compromise his boss, who'd risen by condemning the old regime and the abuses perpetrated by the KGB."

She added, "And Putin's first moves were smooth. He reeled off a string of figures on the tonnes of grain in humanitarian aid being shipped in from Germany, England and France. 'There is no need for worry,' he said.

"It sounds like he was already up-and-running right from when he was first put in charge, " said Alya.

Irina nodded, "We can all learn from how Putin operated. In Dresden they described him as unremarkable. Revisionism presents Dresden as a sleepy backwater where Putin could operate, building up his supporters yet with links to the German underworld. He was laying the foundations for what was to happen on my watch, the waves from which are still lashing the shores of Europe and America right into the 2020s."

Bellevue Hotel, Dresden

Irina continued, "But I've some first-hand experience of seeing Putin in Dresden. One time we had a secret mission. Putin wanted to go back to Dresden, to meet with some old cronies. I didn't think I'd be invited along, but when they realised I spoke German, they asked me to accompany them. They told me I was not to let on that I spoke German, but to listen out for anything untoward."

"We flew to Dresden and stayed in a hotel close to the river. Apparently, it had been owned by the Stasi and was once the only hotel open to tourists in Dresden. Its smart restaurants, cosy bars and elegant bedrooms were fitted out with hidden cameras and bugs. Visiting businessmen were honey-trapped with prostitutes, filmed in their rooms and then blackmailed into working for the East.

"Some techniques hardly change," observed Alya, "I was recently in a western situation where the honey trap was being used."

"Yes, it is shameful that this goes on, but quite often it is the fastest way to compromise someone."

"Then, one day we took off to a small, dark bar in the Altstadt. I realised that this was the real reason that Putin was back in Dresden. Apparently, it was the bar was where he used to meet his agents. On this occasion he was meeting someone who knew him from the old days. It was a man - about the same age - someone he clearly trusted, and I had the feeling that they had been through a lot together."

"Their conversation was about securing a few loose ends. They talked about how they had cleared out the records from the KGB headquarters and burned most of the files. Apparently, the furnace was stoked so high that it burst open from the heat. But they also talked about some links they had made with the US military. They used Dresden as a recruiting point for both Munich and Baden-Württemberg, where the US Army operated in a couple of huge barracks. Putin was gathering information about NATO, which could part of KGB intelligence.

"They also talked about how the Russians had been 'running on empty' for much of this time until they could develop some new money-making schemes. Putin seemed to check whether the other guy was still on-side - he was, and they talked about a few other people who were involved at the same time. I had the strong feeling that Putin was sounding out 'getting the band back together'."

"That's where Eckhart comes in. He was originally East German, but is now an FSB agent, like you. They transferred Eckhart to Saint Petersburg when Putin moved here. He knows some more of the background from the Dresden days, but he isn't someone that Putin would know or recognise. In fact, he slips neatly under the radar, but don't underestimate him, you'll meet him tomorrow."

"So, you and Eckhart? Are you... close?" Alya looked into Irina's eyes.

"No, not like that, we are professionals. But we have one another's backs."

Deep Cover

Irina continued, "Another aspect of the Dresden operation was that it provided so much cover. Putin was stationed there away from the prying eyes of Berlin. Once again, he could learn the moves that he would need when in Saint Petersburg and even in Moscow."

"Is that when he first became involved with the Red Army Faction?" asked Alya.

"That's right," said Irina, "He knew the far-left Red Army Faction could create terror across the West. He understood the power of asymmetric warfare and could see how it could tilt world affairs. I guess it is different now, using more cyber means and fewer bombs to get the results he wants."

"But did Putin know about the West German bombs planted by Libya?" asked Alya.

"I never heard about that directly," answered Irina, "but I heard that one Stasi counter-intelligence officer was horrified at the terror starting to reach West Germany. He tried to disrupt the bombing plots of a group of

Libyans that had become active in West Berlin, but was told to back off by Stasi chief Erich Mielke.

"Mielke said we should concern ourselves with catching American spies and not bother our Libyan friends. Later a bomb went off at a discothèque popular with American soldiers in West Berlin. It killed three US servicemen and one civilian, and injured hundreds more."

"Yes, we were always told back at Academy that America was the arch-enemy," said Alya, "I can see how this could have happened."

"... And for that matter, I assume that the KGB knew in advance about the bomb?" asked Alya.

"Yes," answered Irina, "The KGB were aware of the bombers and how they had smuggled their weapons into Berlin. There was a sentiment that in today's world, when nuclear arms have made military force obsolete, terrorism should become the KGB's main weapon."

"There was another bombing," continued Irina, "This one was talked about in meetings I attended."

" The Red Army Faction tried to disrupt West Germany in a series of vicious bomb attacks, their activities became a key part of KGB attempts to disrupt and destabilise the West. As the end loomed for Soviet power and the German Democratic Republic, it's possible that they became a weapon to protect the interests of the KGB.

"One possible such attack came just weeks after the Berlin Wall's fall. Alfred Herrhausen, chairman of Deutsche Bank, was setting off from his home in Bad Homburg, Frankfurt, for his daily drive to work. The first car in his three-car convoy was already heading down the road that was his usual route. But as Herrhausen's car sped to follow, a grenade containing 150 pounds of explosives tore through his armoured limousine, killing him instantly. The detonator that set off the grenade had been triggered when the limousine drove through a ray of infrared light beamed across the road.

"State sponsored?" asked Alya.

"Presumed State cultivated," answered Irina, "Stasi officers were at the Red Army Faction training camps where members were instructed in the detonation of bomb devices through photo-electric beams just like the one used in the Herrhausen attack."

Hydra headed

"They attached me to his security detail from early on," continued Irina, "I was quite a hot-shot security member in those days - my codename was Amur - named after the leopard."

"That's a cool codename," said Alya, "I ran into a couple called Puffin and Auk recently."

"Low level - they must have been," said Irina, "but you know something, the once famous Amur leopard is becoming an endangered species nowadays - I'm not sure of the symbolism."

Alya smiled, "Well my codename has been of a centuries extinct character! Archangel!"

"Yes, but yours brings down a mighty sword against the devil," answered Irina.

"Well, I suppose it's slightly better than jumping off a cliff like an auk or a puffin!" grinned Alya.

"So, what happened when you first met him?" asked Alya.

"Putin? He seemed to be somewhat in shock about what he had returned to," answered Irina., "The empire had imploded and he could see the wreckage everywhere he looked in Saint Petersburg."

"It wasn't just Saint Petersburg?" queried Alya, "Surely he could also see the decline of the entire Soviet Union? - I mean citizens rebelling against communism, the end of the Berlin Wall, the collapse of the Warsaw Pact? - Even Gorbachov being led into further compromises by western leaders?"

"Yes, all of that," answered Irina, "But then Boris Yeltsin made an error in the way he broke up the KGB. Putin had already built some of his network by this time, and the emerging new form was like something from mythology, with multiple heads matching the four areas that it had been chopped into."

"It played into a new shadowland for Putin, which I suppose he could leverage from his friends in many places?" suggested Alya.

"That's exactly right, and it's what I increasingly saw in my duties to provide him with security cover," answered Irina.

"But look," said Irina, "It's getting late, let me walk you back to your hotel. It's only ten minutes from here."

"I came by taxi," said Alya, "I thought we went around in a big loop. I think it took me ten minutes in the car."

"Yes, but we can walk back the short way, then tomorrow we can meet Eckhart and plan our next few weeks of travel. I can also brief you on the main mission, with Eckhart present."

Alya smiled and Irina called across to the waiter. Irina picked up the bill and paid the waiter.

"Thank you," said Alya and they both put on coats to walk outside into snow-covered streets.

Backwater

"Ah, the snow," said Alya, "This is how I remember Russia, and for that matter Iceland,"

A gentle snow was falling. Sounds were deadened. Alya was glad she had put on boots.

"Ah yes, you were originally from Reykjavik," said Irina, "I guess you are toughened to the elements? - And wear those sensible Sorels"

"I should be - toughened - but I suppose London, Paris and Amsterdam have softened me somewhat," said Alya.

They crunched along the wide Nevsky Prospekt and after brief time Irina diverted them to the right into another street.

"This practically leads back to the Four Seasons," she said, "You are extremely well-positioned in the city."

"I learned that from a friend of mine," said Alya, thinking of Chuck Manners. "He always finds a well-positioned hotel."

They walked further and Irina continued, "Putin had a nickname when he first arrived here, too: it was Volodya or 'little Vladimir', which I think he'd acquired when he was in Dresden.

"The rumour was that he'd been friendly with the Dresden Stasi and that the Stasi's lieutenant-colonel knew everyone in town and oversaw organising safe houses and secret apartments for agents and informants, and for procuring goods for the Soviet 'friends'. Putin learned some Stasi tradecraft which he used to such devastating effect in Saint Petersburg."

"Is that how Saint Petersburg became the home of so much illicit trade?" asked Alya.

"That's right," answered Irina, "The KGB was recruiting agents in companies like Siemens, Bayer, Messerschmidt and Thyssen. Putin was involved, initially through the Dresden Stasi, but increasingly in his own right. There was a firm called VEB Robotron, which made computers for East Germany right in Dresden. They had to get the plans and parts from the West and lured western businessmen to their offices and beyond."

"Early sleaze and smuggling?" asked Alya.

"You could say that, I was often on duty at business meetings which seemed to comprise about ten minutes of business talk followed by a half an hour of discussion of the evening's entertainment."

She pointed towards the hotel, "Look, there you are, back already... Yes, sometimes Putin and his friends would all drink too much vodka and then reminisce about the old days in Dresden. Curiously, Putin himself would usually go easy, but everyone else... well. That's when I heard about the blueprint for a lot of Putin's money moves. It was a scheme set up by the East German foreign trade ministry. They created the Kommerzielle Koordinierung, with a mission to earn illicit hard currency through smuggling and to bankroll the Stasi acquisition of embargoed technology."

"I've heard of the KoKo, didn't it set up a string of front companies all across Germany, Austria, Switzerland and Liechtenstein?"

"Yes, KoKo answered to the Stasi espionage department and ran those companies with trusted agents. Some of them had multiple identities, who brought in hard currency through smuggling deals and the sale of illicit arms to the Middle East and Africa."

"I know the feeling with the multiple identities!" smiled Alya.

"Yes, me too. But back in those days, the Iron Curtain meant that smuggling became the only way for the eastern bloc to keep up with the rapidly developing achievements of the capitalist West," answered Irina.

"And presumably access to a sea-port like Saint Petersburg meant that Putin could develop similar schemes only much larger in scale?" asked Alya.

"That's right. Look we'll talk some more in the morning, and I'll bring Eckhart along. No hurry though. Make it- say - eleven o'clock. I'd better get used to rock-'n-roll times," Irina smiled, briefly kissed Alya on both cheeks, and then turned to leave.

The Mission

Load up on guns, bring your friends
It's fun to lose and to pretend
She's over-bored and self-assured
…
And I forget just why I taste
Oh yeah, I guess it makes me smile
I found it hard, it's hard to find
Oh well, whatever, never mind
…
Hello, hello, hello, how low
Hello, hello, hello, how low
Hello, hello, hello, how low
Hello, hello, hello
…
With the lights out, it's less dangerous
Here we are now, entertain us
I feel stupid and contagious
Here we are now, entertain us

Nirvana
Chris Novoselic / David Grohl / Kurt Cobain

Dead men tell no tales

Alya was sitting in the Tea Lounge at the hotel. The breakfast was being cleared away, but she thoughtfully ordered a few items for when Irina and Eckhart would arrive.

The waiter smiled, "They are locals?" he asked, "Yes," replied Alya, in Russian, "I guess they will have had some breakfast, but we can't be sure."

"Okay, I'll put something together on one of our 'Tea Platters'," he said, smiling.

A few minutes later Irina appeared with Eckhart. Alya realised that the late start was probably so that Irina had a chance to brief Eckhart about yesterday evening's meeting.

They approached and Alya stood.

"Christina!" said Eckhart, "I'm so pleased to meet you."

He spoke English with a slight American accent. He moved in for a hug and Alya smiled. She thought he was a similar age to Irina but had also kept his shape and fitness. Almost wiry, he looked good in the shirt and loose tie that he'd selected for their meeting. Like Irina, he had a leather coat, although his was longer, reaching to below his knees.

"I guess you'll want to call me Christina now?" she asked.

"Yes, we must be rock-'n-roll about this," answered Eckhart, clearly excited about the prospect.

Irina hugged Christina also, and whispered, "We talked about what we should call you earlier this morning, I hope you don't mind!"

Christina laughed, "I've been called Christina for the last few years, so I was having trouble getting adjusted to Alya, anyway!" she answered.

"Er, what about passports?" asked Eckhart.

"Don't even ask such a thing!" said Irina, " A lady must have her secrets!"

They all laughed, just as the waiter appeared with a tray laden with breakfast.

"Ms Sokolova," he started, in Russian, "Here is your breakfast tray. Can I also bring you some fresh drinks?"

"Yes please," answered Christina, in Russian, "What would you both like?"

They all ordered coffees and the waiter walked away.

"This is a fine hotel, " said Eckhart, "A 19th-century royal palace, right here in the Admiralteysky district.

"You can catch an evening ride along the canals from here, and live like Russian royalty," added Irina.

Christina smiled, "So Irina was telling me that you know more about Volodya and his time in Dresden?" she asked, looking towards Eckhart.

"Ach Ja, I was often on the edge of what he was doing back in those dark days," he said, "I think he learned a lot of his moves when he was hidden away in Dresden and then went on to exploit them here in Saint Petersburg."

"Any examples?" asked Christina.

"Yes, but it is across the whole KGB, instead of just Putin. A case of dead men tell no tales."

He paused and reached for the tray of breakfast pastries.

"Three men held an intimate knowledge of the secret financing systems of the Communist Party at the time the KGB was preparing for the transition to a market economy under Gorbachev's perestroika reforms.

"The innocent sounding Property Department was run by Nikolay Kruchina and Georgy Pavlov. It was thought to have a value of $9 billion although Western experts estimated its foreign holdings at many times more.

"That was because of all the slush funds and the way that money could be marked up and marked down?" asked Christina.

"Yes, there were many ways to hide money or trade 'new lamps for old'"

"But in the first few days after the Communist Party's collapse, Russia's new rulers were surprised to discover that the Party's coffers were nearly empty."

"The money had been shifted offshore? Just like the move of the oligarchs today. Get caught holding cash and someone will be after it," stated Christina.

"Precisely - that's why so many Russians buy London properties and other illiquid assets. They are much harder to 'cash in'," answered Eckhart, "At the time the rumours were that Nikolay Kruchina had worked with officials to siphon billions of roubles and other currencies through foreign joint ventures hastily set up in the final years of the regime. These were the filter companies set up in Germany and other countries. It's a move that Putin understood only too well."

Irina interrupted, "And Putin used the same moves on his rise to the top. He played it out first here in Saint Petersburg, but then carried the book of tricks back to Moscow."

Eckhart continued, "Now there were Russian prosecutors investigating what had happened to the Party funds- vaued at hundreds of millions of dollars.

"Oh yes, and a few days earlier, the attempted coup by Communist hard-liners seeking to preserve Soviet power had collapsed in failure. The institutions Kruchina served were being dismantled in front of his eyes."

"Yeltsin had moved in to break things up?" asked Christina.

Eckhard nodded, "Yes, the pro- democratic Russian leader Boris Yeltsin signed a decree, broadcast live, suspending the Soviet Communist Party and ending its decades of rule. It was a big deal here. Yeltsin's defiant stance against the hard-line leaders of the attempted coup had put him firmly in the ascendant. "

"Yes and Yeltsin was going to kick over some tables," said Irina.

"That's right," said Eckhart, "Boris Yeltsin by far eclipsed Gorbachev, who timidly watched as Yeltsin addressed the Russian parliament. Arguing that the Communist Party was to blame for the illegal coup, Yeltsin ordered that the sprawling, warren of the Party's Central Headquarters on Moscow's Old Square be sealed."

Christina interrupted, "But Putin had been a couple of steps ahead of this. He'd kept all his papers in Dresden and then burned them, along with the papers of others who were later to be his allies."

Irina said, "That's right, although most of it is impossible to prove, except what Putin boasted on the record about - you know - the furnace exploding."

Eckhart continued, "But in Old Square's hundreds of rooms there were filed the secrets of the Soviet Union's vast financial empire, a network that spanned thousands of administrative buildings, hotels, dachas and sanatoriums, as well as the Party's hard-currency bank accounts and untold hundreds, perhaps thousands, of foreign firms set up as joint ventures in the dying days of the regime.

"Through these bank accounts and other connected firms, the strategic operations of the Communist Party abroad – and those of allied political parties had been funded.

"It was the engine room of the Soviet struggle for supremacy against the West. This was the empire that Kruchina had administered as the chief of the Communist Party's property department since 1983. Its sudden sealing felt like a symbol of all that was lost. "

Irina's asked, "You know what is coming, don't you?"

"A mysterious disappearance or death?" asked Christina.

Eckhart continued, "Yes, exactly; you know the old KGB moves, Christina Nott. Kruchina must have known that his days were numbered. He went back to his flat in the closely-guarded compound for the Party elite. Kruchina's wife went to bed leaving her troubled husband alone to sleep on the couch.

"Next morning she was awoken by a knock on her door. It was the KGB security man for the building. Her husband, she was told, had fallen to his death from the window of their seventh- floor flat."

"Fell or was pushed?" asked Christina, "It's too much like basic GRU tactics."

Eckhart continued, "Yes, you are ahead of us, Christina. The security man said he'd discovered a crumpled note lying on the pavement next to Kruchina's body. 'I'm not a conspirator,' it said. 'But I'm a coward. Please tell the Soviet people this.' "

"Hmm - a little staged? Why on the pavement? It doesn't ring true." Said Christina.

"Well, the KGB immediately declared his death a suicide. But to this day, no one knows what exactly happened –

or if they do, they are not willing to tell," answered Eckhart.

"You said three people...Three deaths?" asked Christina.

"Yes, the same thing happened to Kruchina's predecessor from the property department. Georgy Pavlov also fell to his death from the window of his flat. It was also recorded as a suicide.

"The same pattern?" asked Christina.

Eckhart continued, "Yes, and then, days after Pavlov's death, another high- ranking member of the Party's financial machine fell to his death from his balcony. This time it was the American Section chief of the Communist Party's international department, Dmitry Lissovolik. Again, it was recorded as a suicide.

Irina added, "These three all knew about the money – but no-one else knew where it had been hidden. And 'someone' was learning how to cover tracks."

"So somewhere there is still a lot of hidden Soviet money in play?" asked Christina.

Purloined in Petrograd

"Now it's a mystery, that's for sure and I'm sure it leads somewhere," said Christina, "but I thought we'd be talking about the other mystery - about my upcoming tour. How do I get musicians? Who will I be performing with? The basics..."

"Well, we want to check something with you first," said Irina.

Christina noticed that Irina had held out her hand to Eckhart. She noticed him squeeze it.

"What? What?" asked Christina.

"We've only just met you, but think we know quite a lot about you," said Irina, "You seemed to break away from the conventional FSB roles and then move into a kind of freelance work."

"That's right - my Pabbi - er father- was also an agent - he'd have been KGB after he finished being a jet plane pilot. I was encouraged into the life because my father could get a highly prestigious transfer to Arkhangelsk. I was trained there to be a good agent and did many missions - mainly security for the FSB, sometimes supporting the GRU. Eventually, after couple of crazy ones, I quit, but the FSB made me one of their offers - you know the kind you can't refuse.

"They said they'd pay me well to stay as a sleeper. They didn't put it like that exactly, but I realised that it must be a set of standard moves for agents that had seen a lot of active service. The jokes about returning to Leningrad to be a taxi-driver didn't exactly apply to me," Christina paused and looked towards them both. She decided that Irina had fibbed about them not being a couple.

"Oh, sorry, I realise we are IN Leningrad right now! But there's something you want to ask me. I can tell," asked Christina again.

Irina hesitated, then said, "Okay, it's this. We are both ready to get out. Finish with the FSB. We see this mission as our best chance. It's global, it has a seasoned professional agent involved- you - but an agent that has already made the transition. And one who has a ferocious reputation. Look we need to know if we can trust you...We are putting our future in your hands."

"Are you two in love?" asked Christina, bluntly.

Irina shifted in her chair, "You mean after what I said yesterday night?"

Christina nodded.

"Yes we are," answered Eckhart, "We've been together for ten years. We can't tell the FSB or they will reduce our allowances."

Christina stifled a laugh, "Sorry - but it is so practical of you both! I must try to put my Russian head back on."

Irina continued, "The reason we want to get out is similar to yours, but we don't have any money behind us. We've been on Russian pay scales for years. It's barely enough to be able to share an apartment here in Sankt Petersburg."

"How did you manage it?" asked Eckhart.

"To get out? I was lucky and took the breaks," said Christina, "Now I am comfortable and can pretty much choose where I operate. That is, until the FSB switches their big magnet back on again."

"But wait. Is that why you are telling me so much about Putin and his money? You have some kind of a plan?" asked Christina.

"That's right," said Irina, "Now we are putting ourselves at your mercy. You could tell the FSB about us and that would be our end."

"Okay, but we need a codeword, " said Christina.

"Money Tree," said Irina.

"You've been thinking about this, but it's a bit too obvious if it comes up in conversation. Let's think...Money Tree - *денежное дерево* - *denezhnoye derevo*... Okay, how about 'Denis' as the codeword? Short for Denis Derevo?"

She could see Irina and Eckhart looking relieved as she answered them.

"...And see, we all seem to get along well together" answered Christina,

She raised her coffee cup and the three of them chinked their cups together – "To Denis!"

"Let's see - '*Lovers in Petrograd*', no wait a minute '*Lovers in Leningrad*'...or maybe that's not so commercial," she smiled towards them, "See I'm already thinking of a lyric title."

"You won't know this one, I doubt:

"It was late one night
  I was awoken by the telephone
  I heard a strangled cry on the end of the line.

Purloined in Petrograd.
  They were suspicious of where your loyalties lay.

So, I paid off a bureaucrat
  To convince your captors they're to secret you away

And at the gate of the embassy
  Our hands met through the bars
  As your whisper stilled my heart.

No, they'll never catch me now
  No, they'll never catch me
  No, they cannot catch me now."

"That's amazing, did you just make that up?" asked Eckhart.

"No, it's from a band called the Decemberists." answered Christina.

"What like the Decembrists? - Life goes full circle!" exclaimed Eckhart, "The Russian army officers in Peter's Square led about 3,000 soldiers in a protest against Tsar Nicholas I's grab of the throne when his elder brother Constantine removed himself from the line of succession"!"

Irina added, "And because these events occurred in December, the rebels were called the Decembrists Декабристы : Dekabristy."

"...And Peter's Square is literally outside of this hotel! - You must have seen the bronze horseman! - that's Peter the Great!" said Eckhart.

"Let's take it as a sign," said Christina.

"Okay," said Irina, "You'll work with us then?"

Christina looked at them both, still holding hands. "In for a penny, in for a rouble!" she answered.

About a band

I'm not one of those who left their land
To the mercy of the enemy.
I was deaf to their gross flattery.
I won't grant them my songs.

But to me the exile's always wretched,
Like a convict, or a patient.
Wanderer your road is dark,
And the bread of strangers tastes bitter.

But in the blinding smoke, the flames,
Destroying the remains of youth,
We have refused to evade
A single blow against ourselves.

And we know that in the final reckoning,
Each hour will stand justified…
No people on earth shed fewer tears,
Are simpler, or more filled with pride.

Anna Akhmatova - 1922

Talking about... Pop Music.

"Let's talk something about the music," said Christina.

"Well, we 've got you a tour, " said Eckhart triumphantly, "It goes to the right places, where we need to go."

"And where's that?" asked Christina.

"Tokyo, then to the USA, to the west coast. To play in LA and then Seattle. You are supporting another band."

"Who are the other band?" asked Christina.

"Erebus," answered Eckhart.

"Erebus?" asked Christina.

"Yes, they are Canadians, who play quite often around Europe. They are quite a dark band."

"Hmm," said Christina, "It's not my obvious audience, I don't think?"

"No, we had to get a band that would tour where we need to go. They listened to some of your tracks, saw a video that you'd made of Hey DJ and said they'd include you in the tour. Their manager is a Brit and said he'd heard of you. They are playing some pretty large stadiums, you know."

"Okay, but what about the practicalities of a band?" asked Christina, "Most of the musicians I've worked with do sessions and wouldn't want to be on a full-time tour."

"Taken care of," explained Eckhart, "We found another band called Jallie T and they've said they will do the tour."

"Wait a moment, I've heard of Jallie T - she's an experimental electro-pop singer and has sometimes tours herself," said Christina.

"That's right," answered Eckhart, " Jallie T is a singer and a small band - electro-fringe. Drums, bass, guitar and synths."

Christina wondered at Eckhart describing electro-fringe. He'd obviously read it somewhere.

"Yes, well won't that be the package on offer?" asked Christina, somewhat confused, "I can hardly break into another singer's band and take it over. And wait a minute - I think Jallie T is Canadian too. I guess the other band - Erebus might even know her."

"Well, it has all been agreed, " answered Eckhart, " You are the act and Jallie T's band is to support you on stage. Jallie T can sing too if she wants."

Christina was quietly seething. "This is all wrong," she said, " I can't just hijack another singer's band like that."

"Jallie T is cool about it. She has already said how much she likes you and that she knows your music attracts a wider following than her own brand of edginess. She thinks it will be better for Erebus to have a mainstream act rather than her quirkiness."

"That all seems pretty magnanimous of her," answered Christina.

"Yes - and the rich fees and expenses helped too." added Eckhart., "You know, we brought her and the band here to Saint Petersburg too, so the you can have some rehearsal time together."

"And where can we rehearse then?" asked Christina.

"It's taken care of. There's a few studios around here, mainly because we are quite close to the University district, but the one I've selected is very modern and has some good spaces. They can be trusted not to rip off your work too."

Christina looked surprised.

"Yes, there's still a healthy business in re-cutting original tracks here. Not remixes, pure bootlegs from masters. This studio has some special arrangements because it also provides some services to the FSB."

"What? Like the bad old days?" asked Christina, surprised.

"Yes, a lot of Saint Petersburg is still wired up, from the KGB days and then Putin's time in the city," answered Irina, "Remember yesterday I was cautious at the Literary Cafe?"

Shrike

"So when do I get to meet Jallie T?" asked Christina.

"Well, she, and the band, are already in town," answered Eckhart, "They started rehearsals yesterday."

"Okay, so can I get along to the studio?" asked Christina.

"Yes, they wanted to get a couple of your tracks down before you showed up," answered Irina.

"Well, I've arranged to meet them tomorrow, with all of us, for a run-through of several tracks," answered Eckhart, " I hope that is okay? I thought then we could go somewhere - to a bar- and you could get to know them all."

"Fine," answered Christina, "So can you tell me the address for the studio?"

"Oh, sure," answered Eckhart., "It's 19 Gorokhovaya, about ten minutes on foot from here."

"It's a similar distance to yesterday's cafe," explained Irina, "You remember when we turned right at Gorokhovaya Street? By the Georgia restaurant? If we'd turned left there instead and crossed over the little bridge across the Moyka River, then it would be on the right-hand side. It's a green stone building, and there's a souvenir shop in the same block."

"That's fine," said Christina, "It can wait until tomorrow, when we all go along together. So now, tell me about this other business?"

"Well, we had a kind of plan. More an idea, we'd like to get to some of the money left behind in Sankt Petersburg."

"Most of it was unaccounted for, and is somehow buried away in various banks. We're uniquely placed to find it, and to move it to somewhere more useful," explained Irina.

"Yes, but it is very dangerous to mess with the Kremlin," replied Christina, "This had better be a good plan."

"Its beauty is that it needs access to funds from overseas, and we will be travelling extensively for the next couple of months," said Eckhart.

Yes, we'll be travelling but we will also be very traceable," replied Christina, "Do you have any idea how difficult this will be? "

"That's why we wanted you to help us," replied Irina.

"Okay, make me a couple of promises about this right now. Nothing by email and nothing by phone. We'll also need secondaries - you know - burner phones. But they will need to look like our regular ones."

Irina looked at Eckhart. They nodded to one another.

"Agreed, but please remember we don't have the money that you are used to in western operations."

"Let me worry about that," said Christina, "And to make it fair, what is my cut?"

"Oh yes, we thought you should get one third of whatever we make. We'd be like three equal partners."

"That seems fair," said Christina, "Thank you for not making it more difficult than it needs to be."

"If we are to trust one another, then we should start on an even basis," answered Eckhart.

"How much will we need to do this thing?" asked Christina.

"We think it will be tens of thousands of dollars, " answered Eckhart, "We have some, but we'd need to ask you for some as well."

"Ha, Pay to Play," smiled Christina., "How much are we getting for the tour?"

"Tens of thousands," answered Irina,

"So I'll be working on this tour for my FSB pay, assuming I front the rest of the cash from the tour fees?" said Christina.

"I'm afraid so," answered Eckhart sheepishly. Christina didn't let on that she had a multiplicity of sources of cash from her various escapades. Eckhart and Irina might be her new friends, but they didn't need to know everything.

"Okay, I guess you know I have an agent?" asked Christina, thinking of Clare, from the Triangle.

"We were hoping to keep this between the three of us," answered Eckhart.

"No, Clare is a vital part of my way of working. She will have to know. And she can bring in other highly trusted resources if we need them. I'm afraid that part is non-negotiable."

Irina and Eckhart looked at one another again, there was a longer pause and then Irina said, "Agreed."

"You'll need to explain more about the finances to me then," said Christina.

Irina's phone rang, "I need to take this," she said. She stood and walked towards the restaurant's entrance.

"It's probably our controller," said Eckhart, "Not Blackbird, we have another one - called *Sorokoput*"

"Hmm, - shrike - 'the butcherbird' ," said Christina, "That controller doesn't sound very friendly."

"We've known her for fifteen years, I even think she knows about the two of us, but has turned a blind eye to it," answered Eckhart.

Irina returned, "We need to go, we've been given an instruction to be somewhere this afternoon."

Christina nodded. Eckhart and Christina stood, they hugged their farewells, and Irina and Eckhart left the restaurant. Christina noticed that the suited man who had been working on his laptop hurriedly packed and left shortly after them.

Meet the Band

Christina looked back to the breakfast platter. Somehow, between them, they had eaten everything except a couple of strawberries. She gestured to the waiter, who smiled and then brought a machine across.

"That's okay, please charge it to my room," answered Christina, signing the small paper he produced.

She left the restaurant and walked to the small hotel shop. She could see what she was looking for, even in the shop window. She bought three of the item and had them each gift wrapped by the woman serving. She'd pay cash for this, instead of charging the items to her room.

Then into the street. The hotel area had been cleared of snow, but she could feel the wind. It reminded her of Reykjavik, where it could look good outside until one got there. The so called 'window weather'.

She pulled her coat tight and looked around. Ten minutes. That's all it would take to get to the studio where she could meet her new band.

Now she had to find the right streets, which somehow looked busier and different in daylight.

...

Soon she could see the small hump in the road denoting the bridge across the river. She knew it could not be far now. A couple of times she had turned around to look to see whether she was being followed, like she assumed Irina and Eckhart were.

She didn't see anyone, and the cars were all moving too quickly for her to be under some kind of mobile surveillance.

In the distance she could see the green-painted frontage of the building that Irina had described and as she approached it, she also noticed a souvenir shop. She looked around for a sign to the recording studio, but in the end had to resort to visiting the souvenir shop to enquire where the studio was located.

"It's through the gates, in a side entrance," explained the man in the shop.

"I'll take one of those tee-shirts, please," asked Christina, pointing to the Roscosmos shirt," In small."

The man used a pole to retrieve the tee shirt from an upper shelf. He smiled, and Christina wondered how she would be able to put it on. She was going to adapt her appearance to being with the band.

"I'd like to wear it," she asked, "Somewhere to change?"

The man pointed to a small try-on area, and Christina walked across, closed the curtain and adjusted her appearance. She emerged in the tee-shirt and with her hair pulled back into a couple of scrunchies.

"You look fantastic," said the man. Christina knew he didn't need to say anything, so she assumed the new look worked.

Then, she made her way outside and around through the gate, to where the studios were located.

This time she had to be buzzed in. She explained in Russian who she was and the door was soon opened. She walked in and could hear a muffled band sound coming from one of the rooms. It was a modern facility and she found a long haired guy sitting at a kind of reception desk.

"Hi," he said in Russian, "You must be Christina Nott? Your band are in Studio A. That's some cool music, by the way."

She smiled, "Always keep the front desk onside," flashed through her mind from the days of Arkhangelsk training.

"I'm Sacha," he said, as he card-swiped her through into the studio area. Christina noticed he had his access card on a lanyard. She'd need to get one of those.

...

Inside, she could hear the band. They were playing 'Body all over you' and a vocalist was making a pretty good job of the lyric.

She tapped gently on the control room door and entered.

"Hi, I'm Christina," she said, in English.

"Hey, Christina, we were not expecting you until tomorrow!" - a Canadian accent, the guy with short tidy-looking hair and a green camouflage t-shirt looked up and smiled.

"They're just finishing this one, let me tell them you are here!"

The fold-back was playing the music in the control room, and Christina thought it a good replica of one of her songs. Through the glass she could see the band.

"Let's see - I'm Lucas and in there are Jallie T that's Alex - on vocals, Ellie on bass, Nate - that's Nathan on lead guitar and, Raff - that's Raphael on drums. Ellie plays synth too, as does Jallie.," he explained.

The singer - Jallie T - with her long hair, highlighted just at the front, and huge sun shades, was singing and moving. Christina could see they had set up like a stage act, rather than for a recording.

The song ended.

"Hey, everyone, Christina's just arrived! I'm sending her in!"

There were whoops and claps as Christina entered the room. Jallie T walked over and stretched out her arms.

"Thank you, thank you - and hey that is one cool T-shirt. I love your look - the hair and everything! - What does that say - Roscosmos - what does it mean?

Christina smiled back - "I think I should be thanking you - prepared to learn all my numbers and come on this trip.

And RosCosmos is the Russian Space Program - like NASA. - See there's a logo." Christina was suddenly aware that the whole band was staring at her chest.

"Oh, come on, let's get introduced!" said Christina to break the moment.

Jallie T said, "You know something, we've hardly gone further than Seattle and Missoula before we got this gig. We're all from around Vancouver. Except Ellie that is, she's British, from London."

"Yes, I'm Ellie, from Islington, London. I play bass and keys."

"I know Islington, I used to be based in Hoxton - well, we called it Hoxditch - not so far from the canal."

"We were practically neighbours, then!" answered Ellie.

"And I'm Nate - Nathan - as you can tell by this instrument I'm holding I play guitar! And I'm from Vancouver all my life."

"Yes, and I'm Raff - that's Raphael, I started out in Montreal, but then my parents moved, first to Calgary and then to Vancouver. My father was in the oil business and used to get moved around."

"Je suppose que tu parles assez bien le français aussi?" asked Christina

"C'était ma première langue - vivant dans la partie française du Canada. Où est-ce que vous l'avez appris?"

Christina switched back to English, "Yes I thought French would be your first language. To answer your question, I spent some time in Paris, so I suppose I speak Parisienne rather than French!"

The others laughed. "Okay, we'll need to watch what we say around Christina."

"And I see you have already met Lucas - Nothing would work without Lucas. He's the genius that keeps us all on the road."

"Well, I heard that last number. You are all excellent, and I like Jallie's twist on the song - Er is it all right to call you Jallie?"

"You can call me Alex, if you like," she said, "my original name is Alexandra, so you can see how I shortened it - My middle name is Jayne and my last name is Tremblay. So that's how I got to Jallie T."

"Well my name is Christina...Christina Nott. Very straightforward."

Alex said, "So, guys, I think we should ask Christina to join in with a number and then maybe we should find a nearby bar where we can talk!"

"Yes, 'Body all over mine' seems like a good place to start..." said Christina.

Ellie struck up the bass riff and Christina started up the lyric.

They played a few bars of the track with Christina singing and then she signalled for them to stop.

"Why stop? - That was terrific," said Alex. The band nodded.

"Do you have the lyric sheet?- I forget some of the words," asked Christina sheepishly, "And hey, you play the song the way it is intended. I love that baseline and the way the other instruments come into the mix."

"And you seemed to be doing pretty good too!"

"Yes, it's changing gears into singing, it's been a while, you know."

"Manuka," said Ellie, "We use manuka honey to help the vocal chords!"

"Rather than whiskey!" laughed Christina, feigning surprise.

Ellie started the bass riff again.

Christina could see Lucas in the control room giving a thumbs up.

Rehearsal

Two hours of rehearsal time passed in a flash. They had tried several of Christina's songs and even tried one of Jallie T's numbers.

"If we had a recording of this it would make a sensational live album!" said Lucas.

"I was told that this place is secure from bootleggers and similar," said Christina.

"Yes - we were told almost under pain of death not to fool around in here," said Jallie T.

"Come on then, let's find a bar," said Nate.

Outside, by the entrance desk, Christina asked Sacha about bars in the area. She spoke Russian to him and he told her about a good bar that he went to sometimes and that also played live music.

"It's called the Commode," he added.

Christina decided it was better to keep quiet about the exact name, at least until they got there.

"I didn't know you could speak Russian as well!" said Alex.

"It'd be a very long story; probably a novel" replied Christina, "Look, Sacha has told me where the bar is, we can get there on foot in a few minutes."

"Excellent," said Nate, "Assuming we can find our way back out of here!"

"You guys go on ahead, I'll finish the wrap up here for the evening," said Lucas.

Christina said something to Sacha, who nodded.

"Sacha says he'll join us in the bar and show Lucas how to get there."

"It will be my pleasure," said Sacha in good English.

Commode

It was a few minutes along the street to the bar. They entered, and it was already busy. Nate spotted a bench-seated area and a round table and jostled everyone over to it.

"Christina, Alex, you go in the middle, we'll surround you!"

"Christina and Alex squeezed into the table area and moved along to the middle of the seats. The others, except Nate, followed, and they were soon established. Nate collected drink orders and headed for the bar.

"I rarely drink when I'm singing," said Alex," I hope it doesn't seem like an affectation!"

"No, I agree, it is too easy to get pulled into things," agreed Christina, "So - thank you again, but I still don't really understand why you are doing this?"

"I can understand your feelings about this but, let's be honest, our chance to get a 'world tour' is pretty slim right now. We've only just started out and despite being good - we think - our audience is very niche. This gives us a great way to jump-start our touring and learn some of the moves."

"Is it coincidence that you are supporting Erebus?" asked Christina, "I notice they are also from Vancouver?"

"You are good, Christina! My partner is Marco Bouchard, who is the singer for Erebus. This is also a great way for us to be together while his band is on the road - although he is still in Vancouver at the moment."

"And what about the rest of you?" asked Christina.

"Think about it, a road trip to Russia, Japan, Australia and California, all paid for, playing stadium level gigs. It's a dream come true."

"Since you put it like that!" said Christina.

"Something I wanted to ask," said Alex, "Would you mind if we worked one of my songs into the set list? - I'd love to be able to say that I've performed something for our PR and so on?"

"Of course," said Christina, "You know what? We should consider two songs. One where you solo and another where we sing together. It will make a great news item too!"

"You are so kind," said Alex, "I can just tell we are all going to get along!"

Christina was wondering why Eckhart had not mentioned Australia when he described the tour.

About the Money

Now I find from week to week the sentence sticking fast
Turn the corner, rub my eyes and hope the world will last
Stranger from another planet welcome to our hole
Just strap on your guitar and we'll play some rock 'n roll

But the money's no good
Just get a grip on yourself
But the money's no good
Just get a grip on yourself

And you should know

Grip: Brian John Duffy / David Greenfield / Hugh Alan Cornwell / Jean Jacques Burnel

How it started

Evening, back in her room in the Four Seasons, Christina was researching Jallie T's band on the internet. Her phone rang. It was Irina.

"I hear you met the band!" she said.

"You are well-informed," replied Christina.

"Da, it was Sacha who told me, he seemed really excited, I understand you all went to a bar afterwards?"

"That's right, it was good to make friends with people. You know, break the ice."

"Yes, I do. Well now we've agreed to work together, I was wondering whether Eckhart and I could visit you in the morning - maybe a little earlier? We could then talk in more detail about our other ideas?"

"Great, it sounds like a plan!"

"Nine o'clock?

"That's fine."

Christina went back to studying Jallie T and her songs and lyrics.

...

The next morning, at just before nine, Irina and Eckhart arrived at the hotel. They all sat to have breakfast together.

"So tell me some more about Putin," asked Christina.

"It's all about power," said Irina, "They get their power and then they hold on to it. They manipulate events into their favour with fear and then use it to extract money. Then they use the money to buy even more power."

"The whole collapse of Russia was an inside job. The men at the top of the KGB's foreign intelligence had decided to blow up their own home."

Eckhart took over, "When the Russian prosecutors came calling in the search for the Communist Party's missing wealth, it was the sentinels of the foreign-intelligence directorate who did everything they could to block them."

Eckhart continued, "Leading the cover-up was Yevgeny Primakov, the former head of the Institute for World Economy, which had quietly been a leading force behind the reform drive, who soon after the coup would be anointed by Yeltsin as Russia's new foreign- intelligence chief.

"Primakov sabotaged the only serious attempt to undo the massive theft that depleted Russia's treasury, and then, under the cover of Soviet emigration they'd also been sending a new group of agents into the West to guard and generate part of the hidden cash networks of Russia's foreign intelligence. Money was being funnelled to other countries and reserved for a later, more covert game. In effect much of the money was successfully stolen, redistributed and then hidden."

Irina added, "It's said that tens of billions of dollars had been transferred to maintain the foreign-intelligence networks of the KGB."

Eckhart continued, "Hundreds of foreign shell companies and Soviet joint ventures had been created in the year leading up to the coup, some founded by the Soviet émigrés, others by the handpicked emissaries from the Komsomol. Remember the KoKo? That was the start of building the network of smaller companies, some of which have been used as purely laundering vehicles for stolen Russian State funds.

"It helps to not have a conscience," continued Eckhart. "When the investigators arrived in Central Office they found piles of foreign passports and stamps from many different countries. There were heaps of other blank travel documents, plus official stamps and visas waiting to be forged. There was a huge photo album filled with pictures of people of all types and races, a selection of wigs and beards, and even rubber moulds for faking fingerprints."

"I guess Blackbird and Sorokoput still have access to this kind of thing nowadays?" speculated Christina,

"Otherwise it would be incredibly difficult to send us on missions."

"That's right," said Eckhart, "But that is the official part of what happens. In those days, there was an increasingly hidden part of the system used for personal gain."

Irina took over the story, "As an example, one of the International Department's employees had rebelled, and smuggled out what he could.

"He was a whistle-blower and the top-secret documents he managed to extract included details of hundreds of millions of dollars in payments to Communist-linked parties abroad.

Eckhart took over, "It showed the Party was regularly dipping into state coffers to fund its political and influence operations abroad. It is a crime against Soviet law. The Party's operations should have been funded from the donations it collected from members, not from state coffers."

Eckhart continued, "The whistle-blowing tripped a further line of investigation. As the team of prosecutors trawled through what remained of the Central Committee's archive, they began to find documents that cast light on the myriad of unofficial, secret schemes via which billions of dollars more in funds seemed to have been siphoned out."

"There were the so-called 'friendly' firms. These were the crony companies at the heart of the vast system of black-market operations that kept the eastern bloc afloat. Those were the ones that Putin had quietly helped to establish."

"These were just fronts, then?" asked Christina.

"Yes," answered Eckhart, "And many of them were involved in the smuggling of embargoed technology. They included the string of front companies that East Germany had deployed across East Germany, Austria, Switzerland and Liechtenstein."

"And it was complex," said Irina, "You have to think of the vast bureaucracy of the Soviets harnessed to these kinds of administrative matters."

Eckhart continued, "Yes, and they involved others in selling much-needed equipment to the Soviets: oil, nuclear power and manufacturing at prices inflated many times over, while the profits were used to fund the activities of the Communist Party.

"Investigators found forty-five of these friendly firms, mostly obscure, " continued Irina, "But there was one well-known name: Robert Maxwell's Pergamon Press, the publishing house that had long been a channel for the sale of Soviet science books to the West.

"Just days before the list was published, Maxwell's body was found floating in the Atlantic Ocean not far from his yacht - it was said to be a heart attack but was really another unexplained death linked to Russian money."

Eckhart continued, "Everything was set up as a big money machine. Other companies working with the Soviet regime that stayed off the radar included huge European firms such as Fiat, Olivetti, Siemens and Thyssen.

"Equipment was supplied, including military goods under the guise of medical equipment. Many firms provided dual-use equipment to the Soviets.

Irina continued, "It wasn't just imports either. Some of them were engaged in barter operations that had been under way for many years.

"The state oil-export monopoly Soyuznefteexport had, for instance, engaged in an elaborate scheme to barter oil for embargoed goods. It had first delivered oil via traders to vast storage reservoirs in Finland, where the oil's origins were disguised before a web of intermediaries sold it on in exchange for embargoed technology and other goods.

Eckhart added, "Everyone was skimming too, taking some money from the top of the pile to put away in a private place."

Graduates

"You remember in 2016, when the FSB graduates from the Moscow Academy took to the streets in a convoy of black Hummers?" asked Irina.

"Yes, how could I forget! I guess most of them are pushing paper at some border crossing now," replied Christina.

"Well, we have to think of those brash individuals as typical of the new guard," continued Irina.

"Yes," said Eckhart, "Hundreds of young businessmen began to set up co-operatives. Most of them sought to import computers or trade in consumer goods."

"The most successful of them, the ones who entered the raw-materials trade or went into banking, were the ones with the most powerful connections. This is where we must start to think of Putin as the conductor of an orchestra."

"Simply put, the businesses knew they needed KGB patronage to be successful."

Eckhart explained, "The law on co-operatives also allowed for the creation of financial or credit businesses – in other words, the creation of banks.

"Some of the state banks even made the creation of new banks a condition of their own provision of loans. It was, of course, a way to move the money around."

Irina added, "There was another loophole in the banking legislation. Once you created a bank, it was possible to trade hard currency. You could could change roubles for dollars at the official fixed state price of sixty-five kopecks to the dollar, and then sell goods at a price worth forty roubles to the dollar."

Eckhart said, "Of course, the profits were enormous."

"Yes," said Irina, "The floodgates had opened for the transfer of hundreds of millions of dollars into accounts abroad through hard-currency trading. Most of it had happened just as the plan for the 'invisible economy' was being signed off, and the secretive, trusted agents (*doverenniye litsa*) were being created.

Christina observed, "Yes, I see the building blocks towards power! Black market, illicit goods and 'services', new banks and favourable trading conditions. Everything was so tilted in favour of the young guns."

"Yes," said Eckhart, "And that's where we believe there is careless money that has been left behind. The young tycoons gained wealth and power under the market reforms launched by Yeltsin's government, and they gradually they began to eclipse their former sponsors in the KGB."

Irina added, "Yes. The new Russia seemed to be emerging, in which the former Komsomol members became brash symbols of the new capitalist age. Corrupt, money seeking, on their way to becoming oligarchs, pushing the old men out of the way."

"Or out of windows, " added Christina.

Eckhart said, "Remember their new mandate: 'Our compass is profit. Our idol is his financial majesty capital.'

"Their goal was to become billionaires and they wanted to demonstrate that there was nothing wrong with getting wealthy after decades in which making a profit was considered a crime. But they enjoyed an inside track to riches from the start."

Irina said, "Yes, this is even closer to where we think there is forgotten money. The new tycoons from the Komsomol benefited most of all when the Yeltsin government granted them access to deep stores of cash, without their having to lift a finger."

Eckhart said, "Instead of having its own treasury, the government authorised the tycoons' banks, including Menatep and Alfa Bank, to hold strategic funds from the Russian budget on deposit.

Irina added, "It was a crazy get-rich-quick scheme for the chosen favourites of the Yeltsin regime. They could direct hundreds of millions of dollars in government funds into high-yielding investments, sometimes even into the privatisation auctions, while the government was left waiting for the disbursal of its funds.

Eckhart continued, "Vital programmes such as defence spending or aid for citizens were delayed or simply unpaid, while the ruthless new bankers fobbed the government off with promissory notes. The government was being bled dry, while the new wolves of the Russian economy concocted elaborate schemes to avoid paying taxes or customs duties."

Christina added, "We must watch out though. These new guard are faster and more adept in the ways of the market than their one-time masters in the KGB."

Eckhart continued, "So then we come to the pivot point, when control of the economy swung irrevocably towards the new tycoons. It came when Russia was entering the year before the first post-Soviet presidential elections, and the government's coffers were empty. Wages and pensions were months in arrears, and Yeltsin's approval ratings were terrifyingly low, at 6 per cent."

Irina added, "The tycoons feared a return to Communism, which would strip them of their fortunes and could even land them in jail. Even more importantly, they'd long been eyeing the crown jewels of Soviet industry, the state's biggest industrial giants. If they could unlock those big assets there would be billions of outflow,"

Eckhart added, "Yes, what they'd acquired so far was small-scale compared to the vast resources still under the control of the state. They needed a scheme to pull through the wealth of Russia to these same tycoons.

"This is where 'loans for shares' came in?" asked Christina, " An original sin of Russia's market transition."

Eckhart nodded, "Yes, it tainted everything, and opened the way for constant threats over the legality of the property the young tycoons acquired at that time."

Christina nodded again, "Yes, it was a massive insider deal that transferred the nation's resource wealth into the young bankers' hands at a knockdown price. I'm still amazed that the rest of the world didn't notice."

"That is the point about the agility of the young tycoons," said Irina, "They were far more financially nimble, and able to access much bigger pools of ready cash through the rapid growth of their banks and the government deposits they held. This was when the young tycoons started outmanoeuvring their former KGB masters."

Eckhart continued, "Most of Soviet industry passed into the hands of the young bankers, in auctions that were widely seen as rigged. They literally stopped people from attending some of the auctions by putting up roadblocks.

"Vladimir Potanin got Nickel and platinum. He acquired a controlling stake in Norilsk Nickel, a sprawling plant high above the Arctic Circle whose profits in 1995 stood at $1.2 billion. He'd done so by extending a loan of just $170 million to the government – and when, as expected, the still cash-strapped government defaulted on the loan after Yeltsin secured his election victory, the way was clear for Potanin to win the stake in an auction for little more than the loan price.

"Mikhail Khodorkovsky had long been targeting Yukos as the oil producer in west Siberia. He took control of it after lending the government $159 million for a 45 per cent stake, and then paying a paltry $150 million in investment for an additional 33 per cent.

"Boris Berezovsky, paid $100 million for Sibneft, another oil producer. He already controlled sales at Russia's biggest carmaker and chaired a bank of his own. "

"And they were still in their early thirties?" asked Christina.

"Yes," answered Eckhart, "Most of these bankers were barely in their thirties, but with the help of sympathetic government officials running the auction process, they were able to secure the foundations of fortunes that within a few years would be worth billions, and then tens of billions, of dollars."

Eckhart continued, "Seven young bankers soon controlled 50 per cent of the nation's economy. Look any one of them up on Google and a whole row of related individuals fills the next line. This was the moment the tycoons were transformed from mere bankers to owners of the biggest assets in the country, with access to some of the most lucrative cash flows."

"They had access to the run rate cash from raw materials and banking?" asked Christina.

"That's right, they all started to reinvent themselves," said Irina, "They acquired real assets. They became much more than banks. These tycoons of Russia's new order were giddy at their new wealth. They were fast becoming oligarchs who held considerable sway over the weakened Yeltsin government."

Eckhart added, "The remaining members of the old-guard security services who had served in government had been ousted amid scandal in the run-up to the presidential elections, It was the climax of their era. The country, it seemed, was theirs."

Irina added a warning, "But the oligarchs forgot to whom they owed a debt. They didn't notice that nearby, in Saint Petersburg, things were being run differently. Here, in Saint Petersburg, forces of the KGB were exerting far greater control, in a city where the economy was tougher and darker, in the violent scrabble for cash. They would need to pay attention or could find themselves violently ousted."

Whistle Blower

"I'm getting a sense of where you'd be finding the money in your plan," said Christina, "Some of the big ticket items were unaccounted for maybe?"

Irina said, "Correct. There's always been a fear culture around the money; you only have to look at what happened to those three men from the property department, or come to think of it, Robert Maxwell."

"What, they all took a dive," said Christina.

"Quite literally they all took a dive - three from windows and one into the Atlantic," said Eckhart.

"Just about everyone has been too frightened to say anything. It is not just fear for themselves, but fear for what might happen to their entire families as well, " said Irina.

Then Eckhart added, "Yes, but there was a lead for us - one person who turned into a witness was Leonid Veselovsky, a former colonel in the foreign-intelligence directorate of the KGB."

"You are trying to 'follow the money'?" asked Christina.

"That's right. Veselovsky was one of a number of top KGB foreign-intelligence operatives drafted in to help manage and hide the Party's property and wealth."

"But this must have been many years ago?" asked Christina.

"It was, but we are sure that the treasure is still out there, buried or in some kind of dubious use," answered Irina.

"Yes, and there's been so much money hidden away, that we only need to tap into a small portion of it and we'll all be rich," commented Eckhart.

Christina smiled, she needed to decide how sensible or delusional these people were.

"These foreign-intelligence officers like Veselovsky were brought in for their knowledge of how Western financial systems worked. And they reported to Kruchina (the first man out of a window)." continued Irina.

"But I don't see any links in this back to Putin?" said Christina.

"Well, hold on for a moment. Something else that the new Party was going to need, was an invisible economy, which could hide the Party's wealth. Putin would need that in Saint Petersburg and then he'd also need it back in Moscow. Remember Putin had also befriended a whole network of people in Dresden. This included links into the old KGB, as well as into the dirty tricks departments of the Stasi. There's a well-known photo of him visiting a tank museum, which shows the alleged depth of the rogues' gallery."

"I see, he was using time in Dresden to build his connections," said Christina, "But he'd need some people here in Saint Petersburg too? - Ideally some that were not too law-abiding?"

"You are getting ahead of yourself," said Irina, "All in good time."

Eckhart continued, "Back to Veselovsky. He was a specialist in international economics and had been transferred in to work on the plan to create an 'invisible economy' for the Party's wealth.

"It was Veselovsky who proposed the system of 'trusted agents', or *doverenniye litsa*, who would hold and manage funds on the Party's behalf.

"He prepared a series of notes for Kruchina with proposals for disguising the Party funds to protect them from confiscation. These included investing them in charitable or social funds, or anonymously in stocks and shares. The process was to be led by the KGB.

"That's what the oligarchs still do today, except it is with their wives and lawyers, rather than other party officials," said Christina.

"Yes, on the one hand these arrangements ensured a stable income independent of the future position of the Party.

"On the other, these shares could be sold at any moment through stock exchanges and then transferred to other spheres to disguise the Party's participation while retaining control."

"So that's why the modern party turned over the old guard," said Christina, "To move the wealth to new, younger owners."

"In order to conduct such measures, there needed to be an urgent selection of trusted custodians to carry out separate points of the programme. In effect secret Party members who could ensure the Party's existence under any conditions.

"That's when Veselovsky came up with the pro-forma that some of the Party members signed, committing to hide funding and keep it secret.

"And the new guard want to prise the agreements out of the old guards' hands - dead or alive."

"And there's the irony, in some cases it is only the dead men who knew where the money was secreted."

"No coincidence that Putin sanctioned off-shore retributions back in 2006, which was a quick way to settle old scores, clean up his stables, and give the hunters some bounty," said Irina.

"That's right, "said Eckhart, "In 2007 Putin made his revisionist intentions known in a speech at a Munich security conference in Germany. He spoke shortly before standing down from the presidency, temporarily, in favour of his protégé Dmitry Medvedev.

"Putin attacked the US's domination of global affairs and reeled off a series of allegations: NATO's expansion; Western "meddling" in Russia's elections; nuclear treaty violations. He was sounding out the first moves of a long game."

"I understand this," said Christina, "better now that when I landed in Sankt Petersburg, but I can't help think that the money you, I mean we, are looking for has been hidden by someone who was subsequently murdered

About a Tour

'You in the west, you think you're playing chess with us. But you are never going to win, because we're not following any rules'

Semion Mogilevich to his lawyer

Clare

Christina was back at her hotel. She called Clare's phone.

"Hi, it's Clare, Christina - How are you? - last thing I heard was that you were packing - er - a suitcase!"

"Enough of those American secret agent jokes, " said Christina, "I'm good and guess what? I'm about to go on a road trip, with a band, as Christina Nott!

"I'd very much like it if you can come long as well, partly for back-up, and partly because you can quickly organise the others back at The Triangle."

"Sure, Christina, exciting! Where are you? I can come over this afternoon to talk."

"Er - I don't think so, I'm in Saint Petersburg, Russia, it's a long story."

"How do I even get to Saint Petersburg?" asked Clare.

"You could fly Aeroflot, but I came here with Lufthansa. They both go via Moscow. The Lufthansa flight has a longer transfer time. 10 hours instead of 7 hours. But you don't see the air-stewards on Lufthansa sweeping water off the luggage racks with a broom."

"Okay, I'll see what I can get. I'll tell the others and then pack and leave - probably tomorrow's flight. What's the weather like?"

"Its cold and snowy, bring grippy boots. I'm in the Four Seasons, so prepare to be pampered,"

"Got it," said Clare.

"Be prepared to move on though," said Christina.

"To where?"

"Tokyo, and then West Coast USA. I'm touring with the 'new' band."

"Okay, I think I'll be using a credit card then," said Clare, "But I'll pack some 'rock chick' items too. How long away?"

"I guess it could be around three weeks."

"For you, darling, I guess I'll just hop onto the plane."

They both laughed.

Rehearsal 2

This time Christina had found her way to the studio with no problems. She had said hello to Sacha on the way in and asked how she could get one of those card swipes so she could get in and out of the studio.

He paused for a moment and then reached into a drawer.

"Here," he said, still speaking Russian, "You can have one now, I'll put it onto a lanyard. Just promise you will return it when you have finished here and maybe sign it out in this book."

He pushed a book towards her and she signed her name "Christina Nott."

You are a great singer," he said, "I didn't recognise you the first time, but it is wonderful to have a proper Russian singer making great pop-music. I think you are probably Russian Pop Royalty! Look - this isn't cool, but can I have a selfie with you?"

"Of course," smiled Christina, "Lets do a couple!"

He found his phone and they did one cheesy photo together.

"Look - let's do one where I'm kissing you on the cheek," smiled Christina, "If you don't mind, that is!"

"Oh no, that would be great!" stuttered Sacha and prepared for the next selfie. "You know something, that is one of the greatest moments of my life!"

Christina smiled again. "You can tell your friends that we are friends," she said. She looked at Sacha who was reeling under her charm offensive.

Next she put the lanyard around her neck, waved the Proximity card at the door and entered the control room.

"What a lovely man," she said referring back to Sacha.

Lucas looked up from the controls. He spotted the lanyard and said, "Christina, I have lanyard lust - how did you get that access badge? An hey, you know something, I've been listening back to some of your tracks from yesterday. They are album quality, you know,"

"Wow, thank you; I thought the two part version of Hey DJ with JallieT came out well, and I loved the way she did 'I can feel my body all over you' ," she said.

"Yes, I thought that was great as well; did you say you were looking for a track that she could do during the show? I reckon that could be the one."

Sacha entered the control room, this time with Jallie T, Ellie, Nate and Raff in tow.

"The band are here, " he announced, "enjoy your rehearsal time."

He exited and they all said hello to Christina.

"We were just talking about the last rehearsal," said Lucas.

"I think you've nailed the musicianship," said Christina, "I worked with some hardened session musicians in Amsterdam a while ago and they took longer to learn tracks than you do!"

"And Jallie T - you are one heck of a singer - I love your look today, by the way!"

"Yours too!" said Jallie, looking at Christina's black leather jacket, beret and dark glasses, "You are channeling a mysterious woman assassin or something?"

"Ah you got me in one, and yours looks like something styled by Vogue!"

"It was! I did a magazine shoot and this was some of the stuff they gave me!" said Alex, clearly excited.

"You should see the swag she got from a shoot for subvrtmag in Toronto," said Ellie, "It was other-worldly. Bright green shiny!"

"All we got were the rotten tee-shirts" laughed Nate, "When we went to Toronto for a gig"

"Yes and it doesn't look all that cool for us all to walk around wearing the same Jallie T shirts!" added Raff, "No offence Jallie,"

"None taken," said Alex, "I feel your pain- did you ever have problems with your record company? They sometimes feel like they are the KGB or something!"

"Mine too," said Christina, savouring the irony.

"You know what, after that I feel like blasting through "I'm a hitman, baby!"

"Yeah," said Nate," A nice stroppy song to bash out some power chords!"

With that, he walked into the studio, picked up the Gibson and punched out the first few chords.

"All Right, Tiger," said Ellie and she wandered into the room, picked up her pearlescent Jaguar bass and joined in the bass-line. Raff looked at Christina, "Come on then, let's show them how its done!" and with that he moved to his conventional drum kit and picked up the beat.

Christina kicked in with the vocals:

don't promise me no promises
  and its the same from me to you
  on the run from love this time
  we both knew what to do

pack my bags, go around the world
  sleep anywhere I please
  you stayed, but didn't wait, in this Chelsea flat
  when I returned at the end of a mission

'cos I'm your hit man, hit man
  always on the run
  yeah I'm your hit man, babe
  always got a diff'rent gun

Then, Jallie T for the second round:

last time in Jakarta when the rain was hot
  I'd been running for the Java Sea
  they came after me with that Mata Hari girl
  but my mind was able to break free

and before that, together in St Petersburg
  we were hiding in that Lit-er-tur-noy Caff
  I'd done the deed, we were holding hands
  that time when we both looked happy

'cos I'm your hit man, hit man
  always on the run
  yeah, I'm your hit man, babe
  always got a diff'rent gun

Christina looked at Jallie T, "Together?" she mouthed, so they did:

even then I could tell that our war was over
  your warmth told more than lies
  a silencer moment of instant truth
  a burst of sun from your deep blue eyes

never promise me your promises
  we both knew just what to do
  still running from love after all this time
  and this time its without you.

cos I'm your hit man, hit man
  always on the run
  yeah I'm your hit man, babe
  always got a diff'rent gun

yeah I'm your hit man, hit man

always on the run

The last sizzle died away from the cymbal. The band looked at one another.

A crackle on the P.A. System, Lucas spoke, "O...M...G...That was brilliant. I loved that organic start. You've got to put this track out! Even as a streaming single!"

Everyone in the rehearsal room laughed. They realised that a piece of magic just occurred. They were a proper band now.

"But hold on, how did you write about Saint Petersburg? And that Cafe? I thought you'd never been here? And when did you write that one?"

"You know, I can remember it most distinctly, February 17th, 2010. It was a bit of a break-up song, actually, just after St. Valentine's Day," answered Christina, "Oh nicely sung too - Jallie T!"

"What you were breaking up from another hit-man? It's brilliantly bonkers!" said Ellie, then noticing Christina's expression, "Oh - I didn't mean anything by that last remark!"

"No, I agree with you. Who in their right mind would write about a hit-man break-up?"

"Let's see, what else have I got by way of break-up songs?...How about French kiss-off?"

Play On, Christina Nott

They all flicked through their notes and found the track. Ellie and Nate struck up a drum and bass rhythm for this one and then Nate chopped in a few chords.

Christina signalled for them to stop.

"Guys, I know this one is another guitar driven one, but I wonder what it would be like to use an acoustic production? Make the lead into an acoustic and wind the bass back until maybe half way through?"

Nate swapped his guitar over; the others waited whilst he positioned himself on a stool.

"From the top, " he said, "3-2-1 and..." The same tune came out, this time with some fiddly embellishments as Nate plucked at the guitar.

Christian moved towards the microphone and began to sing.

The rest of the band nodded their approval and then, after 16 bars, there was a gentle scraping as Raff's drums came in.

Next it was Ellie's bass, dialled right back in the mix.

Jallie added a few quiet harmonies to the last part of the song, which ended with a gentle sigh.

They all looked at one another. There was a frisson of joy in the room, despite the song being another sad one.

"Magical," whispered Jallie T.

"Thank you, guys, I think we achieved an almost perfect arrangement. Nate that was great guitar work, and Ellie and Raff, what a perfectly balanced backbeat. And thank you, Jallie T for drifting those quiet harmonies against my voice."

"These Saint Petersburg recordings will be as famous as The Esher Demos," said Lucas.

"The other thing that is so good is how quickly you are all picking up the songs, I've never seen anything like it!" said Christina.

"Um, we should come clean...We were given your recordings and some lyric sheets a couple of weeks before we flew from Vancouver. They became our obsession during rehearsals in Vancouver," admitted Nate.

Jallie T nodded, "Yes, we called ourselves the 'Christina Nott Really' " for a while - as a joke - you know, the CN tribute band."

"I'm actually rather flattered by that; I've never had a tribute act before!" laughed Christina.

"But what about your money peeps? Aren't they going to show up? Don't they care about the music?" asked Ellie, "It's a bit weird them not being here at all. "

"I know," said Christina, "I wouldn't be surprised if they are both connected into the local scene here in Saint Petersburg. You know that is why we are here, don't you? It is where they both live, so I guess there must be a Russian influence running through all of this?"

Christina was making the back-story run as close to the reality as possible.

"Oh, we thought they were part of your gang," said Alex, "You being part Russian, we'd guessed that they were relatives or friends or something."

"No, I also just met them for the first time here," answered Christina, "They've been telling me about the wild times here in Saint Petersburg over the last 20 years!"

"Sound like there might be another lyric in it!" laughed Alex.

Christina answered her phone. It was Clare.

"I'm here, in the Four Seasons, in my new snow boots."

"Excellent," said Christina, "I'll be back in a couple of hours! Time for you to unwind from the flight!" And then, on cue, in walked Irina and Eckhart. There were greetings as everyone met. Christina realised that the band had already met both of Irina and Eckhart.

"Okay, prepare yourselves for a treat! - Full on music concert!" said Jallie T and the band clicked back to the top of the set and started playing "My body,"

What we'll do on the road

Irina walked outside of the rehearsal studio with Christina.

"That was a great session - absolutely brilliant," she said, " I don't think we will have anything to worry about."

"The band are really good, and Alex - Jallie T - is a fine singer," replied Christina.

"Yes, although she doesn't have some of your 'other' skills," answered Irina.

"Now; I know you have resisted asking me about the main mission, but I think it is time to explain. You will be meeting Ulyanina Karina Rostislavovna - she is the new controller for Saint Petersburg."

"A woman?" asked Christina.

"Yes, someone who has been in active service like both of us, now she runs the desk here in Saint Petersburg. She is to brief us all about the mission."

"Okay, I should explain that my colleague, Clare, just arrived in Saint Petersburg, I'd like the briefing to include her."

"I'll see what we can arrange. Strictly, this is FSB business."

"Clare is someone who I completely trust. You must tell that to Karina."

"I'll tell her, but I can't make guarantees."

"And I won't come along without Clare. It's as simple as that."

Spencer

April 43rd 2000

Today is the day of great triumph. There is a king of Spain. He has been found at last. That king is me. I only discovered this today. Frankly, it all came to me in a flash."

— Nikolai Gogol, Diary of a Madman and Other Stories

Meet the Russians

They all arrived at the building. Irina, Eckhart, Christina and Clare. The building looked anonymous from the outside. There was a wall surrounding a courtyard and an inner building. They had to be buzzed in to walk across the courtyard and then buzzed again to gain entry. Christina noticed that the car parking for the building was underground.

"Some security here. Two layers of entry. A regular fortress?"

"Yes the FSB is very particular about some of its locations."

A security man greeted them at the doorway.

"You are here to see whom?" he asked.

Irina explained in Russian, Christina decided it was better to remain quiet. Clare didn't know what was happening.

"Okay, we can go in now and he will show us the way to Karina Rostislavovna.

They approached an office and the guard swiped them in. "That's the third layer, said Christina, and looking towards the door to Karina Rostislavovna.'s office she added ," And I see there is a fourth."

They were buzzed into what was a large and long office, and could see Karina wait for them by her desk.

"Hello, she said, starting in Russian, "You must be Archangel and Amur," she said, looking towards Christina and Irina, "but I don't think I know you two?"

She looked towards Eckhart and Clare.

"I'm Eckhart, " and "I'm Clare, "came the responses, "A friend of Irina and a friend of Christina,"

Karina gestured for them to sit. She started speaking Russian, "Okay, I'll be briefing you about the mission now. The usual rules. Strictly Confidential. No discussion with anyone outside of this session. "

Christina quickly translated for Clare. She nodded that she knew the score.

Karina switched to speaking English, Christina thought she had a very clear accent, typical of the Home Counties of the United Kingdom. She must have spent time in London.

"I'll speak English so that we can all keep up. This mission is about leverage. We want to increase the leverage we have over a foreign nation. We are using a politician. An American. High profile. It's Logan Spencer."

They all looked at one another.

Karina continued, "I know, Spencer is a controversial character. Popular enough to get American Republican votes, but generally reviled outside of the 'flyover states'.

"Outside of the megaregions of the United States, he is considered great, using his appalling schlock to get his own way.

"The mainly Democrat states and much of the Main Stream Media see him as a threat. We can counter that in some areas with our Russian controlled media outlets, but he doesn't seem to always want to play the right game. It is like he has become confused by his own power."

Karina stood, "Your mission is to remind him how he got his power and the degree of financial and other kompromat we have over him.

"I would call this Spencer Stew," she projected a PowerPoint Slide

Prepare the ingredients

1) Meet Spencer in Tokyo about his new tower. Tell him we want his backing. Offer him a large sum of money, offer this as his salvation.

2) Arrange for Spencer to meet his other backers in L.A. They tell him he is a spent force and that they will back away from the deal.

And another slide, accompanied with a picture of a pot of Russian Winter stew.

"*Zima tushenaya!*" said Christina, "Winter stew!"

"*Solyanka*," said Irina, looking more carefully at the ingredients.

"You can both be right, so long as we find a restaurant that serves it after this!" said Eckhart.

Simmer

3) Let him fret. He'll want the new deal to get money to cover his debts. He'll need to decide how he can handle the possible lack of Russian support.

"Is this where we add the sour cream and the herbs to boost the flavour?" asked Eckhart.

Add a kicker spice.

4) Show Spencer an alternative backer.
Meet him in Seattle. Introduce him to a billionaire technology backer. Show him a way out in exchange for fees. Transfer fees to his account from Kremlin accounts. Compromise him.

"Do you think he will bite?" asked Clare
"With something this tasty?" said Eckhart.

Serve it hot
5) Meet him one more time, maybe in Washington or Miami. Tell him we have the Kompromat. About the money laundering. About the banking theft. About the links to Russian organised crime. That we also know he is about to go under financially.

Enjoy
6) Make Spencer an offer that means he will work for us if we get him into high office. Remind him that he is forever in our debt.

"That's a good plan," said Christina.

"Deceptively simple," said Karina, "Let's hope we don't have too many cooks here."

"But first, I want to take some time to review Spencer's rise to power and high office."

Pavle Darchidze

Karina began, "I'll start by describing to you all a key player. Pavle Darchidze. He has been tasked with snaring a senior American politician."

She pressed a button on her laptop and Darchidze's picture appeared.

"Pavle Darchidze left Russia before the Soviet Union fell, in that wave of repatriation in the early eighties. His supposed marriage to a French national was, by Darchidze's own admission, a fiction.

"Before he left the Soviet Union, he was befriended by two leading lights of Soviet foreign intelligence. First, Yevgeny Primakov the Russian spymaster; and second the former head of Soviet military intelligence in the United States, Mikhail Milshtein who was a good friend.

"Darchidze, an ethnic Georgian, is bespectacled with dark hair and trained as an engineer in Saint Petersburg. In the early days his business was antique smuggling, selling ancient icons, paintings and other valuables into the West.

"That was how it all started, wasn't it?" with basic black-market shipments?" asked Christina.

Karina nodded, "Yes, Darchidze was typical of many. One branch of the then KGB pursued him for his black-market activity, but Russian foreign intelligence cultivated him, before sending him to the West.

"The KGB were preparing for a market transition, as the only way to survive in competition against the West. KGB chief Yury Andropov pushed for the changes, while the old guard fought against it because it could affect their positions of power.

"Putin could see the progressives cultivating agents in the black market and funnelling out antiques and then raw materials through them.

"That's what I was explaining to you the other day," said Irina, "How Putin moved in on Saint Petersburg, opportunistically, using a mix of black market, fear, criminality and then moving into control through shipping, dockside and banking."

Karina nodded, "Yes, it was an obvious move to use organised-crime networks, which sent out representatives in the wave of emigration permitted in the late seventies and early eighties. These people opened trading businesses in Austria and Switzerland, and then deeper into the West."

Karina continued, "The men like Primakov - the spymaster - moved around too. He was now at Moscow's Institute for World Economy, and Mikhail Milshtein was now at the Institute for USA and Canada and pushed the reforms and saw the paths to greater riches and power."

"They had a lot of global trade under their influence," said Clare.

"Yes," said Karina, "When the Soviet Union collapsed under the force of change and the flood of assets into the West, the KGB progressives were prepared. Their agents were already embedded, and the cash networks they'd created were already working under their control."

Karina continued, "But Darchidze would never directly admit that he was part of this process. Although the story about him leaving Russia to join his wife was no more than a cover.

"That same year he'd set up one of the Soviet Union's first joint ventures from his base in Berlin on the Western side of the Wall, which he used for smuggling cigarettes and alcohol to Soviet military bases in the East.

"Darchidze rented a small flat above a casino run by Soviet émigrés just off the Kurfürstendamm, West Berlin's main thoroughfare, and was soon frequenting the grand halls of the Hotel Bristol, near which he set up an office.

"And on the West side of Berlin he had high-level protection, having become friends with the Soviet consul, Rudolf Alexeyev.

"The year the Wall fell, Darchidze attended the victory celebrations in Berlin's Spandau Castle with Alexeyev and other Soviet dignitaries.

"And that's when he met our target, Logan Spencer."

Christina and Clare both gasped as they heard this name. One of the biggest fish in American politics. A noisy and controversial wheeler-dealer politician, who used hate tactics to whip up a crowd.

Karin continued, "Yes, by the time he met Logan Spencer in November 1990, Darchidze had made it. The joint venture he'd set up had expanded into trading computers, and then into construction.

"His contract was to build the first business centre for foreign companies in Moscow, which was to house a French energy major. It was, with hindsight, ridiculous that a Russian builder would construct the offices used by a French oil company. The French would pay for their own additional secret wiring and bugs."

"It delighted his partners in the Soviet foreign ministry. Not only could they keep close watch on their foreign tenants, they would receive huge sums from them too. Darchidze was already a high roller, and when he entered Spencer's Golden Dollar in Atlantic City, he liked what he saw.

"The Golden Dollar was a vast palace of forty-nine storeys dripping with chandeliers and gold, and featured a dome reminiscent of St Basil's, in Moscow. You could say that Spencer liked colourful, but not as much as he liked gold. "

Karina's description was interrupted. A man in a leather coat entered the room. He had a shock of dark hair and was wearing spectacles.

Karina beamed a broad smile toward him and then announced, "But let me introduce you all. He has finally arrived. This man is Pavle Darchidze!"

Clare and Christina stood to shake his hand. Karina hugged him. Eckhart shook his hand, as did Irina. They all introduced themselves.

"Ladies, Gentleman, I am sorry I am late, they delayed my plane in Paris. I've flown from L.A."

Christina noticed he was already speaking effortless English with an American west coast accent.

"Ha, Pavle," said Karina, "You have arrived at just the right time and from the right city. We are just talking about your visit to Atlantic City, when you first met Spencer."

"Karinushka, shall I continue the story?" he grinned and looked around the table.

"In Atlantic City there were hundreds of gaming tables, and elegant lounges, restaurants and bars. I was in the Golden Dollar and saw Spencer for the first time one morning around 3 a.m.

"Suddenly there was Spencer, and around him were dozens of people. He looked shorter than I expected, but with a thick tan and his hair close-cropped to his head. We were there for three or four days, and every night he would appear at 3 or 4 a.m.

"It was a huge operation, and he had spent vast money on the Golden Dollar.

"We were playing in the casino. We already had money by then. We had big money by then. Spencer showed us around; where the cash room was, where the safe was, where the computers were and everything. He lived there, and around him were many beautiful girls.

"I had to use my chance to create the relationship with Spencer. I didn't know how far it would reach nor that it would form the basis of a network of Russian intelligence operatives, tycoons and organised-crime associates that have orbited Spencer almost ever since. Spencer attracts bad guys and illicit schemes and so was a magnet for corruption.

"I was invited to meet Spencer that first evening by a leading player in the Atlantic City casino industry – a lawyer who had drafted New Jersey's casino laws in the early eighties and then become president of one.

"Spencer and his American legal partner were trying to find a way to the much talked about Communist Party wealth.

"My partners and I had all met together earlier in Yalta, on the Crimean Peninsula, and discussed potential investments, including possibly building a Soviet casino there. We realised that the Americans were also 'looking for investments in their casinos', They'd heard the myth of the Party money, and they decided the casinos would be a good home for it.

"There was no deal though because the Americans make their own business too transparent. It would have been obvious that the money came from Russia. But then the lawyer invited me to Atlantic City to meet Spencer. He said Spencer 'knew how to tilt the tables' and could be interested in fast ways to get access to money.

"Knew how to tilt the tables! Something of an understatement for the tax avoiding crooked politician?" questioned Clare.

"You have to remember that nowadays much of America loves Spencer. The idea he would be up to no good doesn't enter their ill-informed heads," said Pavle.

"Spencer had poured so much money – more than $1 billion – into building the Golden Dollar that he was deep in debt and facing bankruptcy. He owed the banks so much money that they were afraid to foreclose on him.

"Spencer said that the casino business was an uphill struggle. He later told Manhattenite Magazine that in 1990 he was $5 billion in debt, with $800 million in personal guarantees.

"But then, two years later, Spencer had achieved a remarkable turnaround. Truly remarkable. He'd reduced his personal guarantees to $100 million by selling off his yachts and planes and had somehow managed a restructuring on the rest of his debts.

"He'd done this by manoeuvring his business through a crafty pre-packaged bankruptcy. He got lucky and was bailed out, but the luck was purely because of Russia. We had two assets because of this. We could use the Casino for money laundering, and we had Spencer on-side.

"We had to use a few Wall Street people to help us get the bondholders to support Spencer, but the end result was a Spencer-badged casino operating in an unregulated part of the USA, available as a vehicle for cleansing Russian money. It was a brilliant scheme.

Clare asked, "Did Spencer know what was happening?"

Pavle replied, "Spencer was not a good businessman. He said he was, but he relied on tricks and cons to get most of his success. He would sue anybody and was prepared to withhold payments. It was his normal way of working. He said if someone attacked him he would attack them back only 100 times as hard. We let him believe his own puffery."

"So, did he know about the laundering?" asked Clare.

Pavle answered, "You know, I expect someone smarter than him told him there was money laundering taking place, but I doubt if he cared as long as the casino house still got its cut of everything.

"In Moscow, word got out, and so soon afterwards Spencer was boasting of record profits for the house several months in a row. He was getting a cut of the Russian money that was being legitimised."

"His cut of the cleansed dirty money?" asked Christina.

"Yes, It was kind of funny, "answered Pavle, "All of the Russian émigrés had been going there in droves almost ever since the Golden Dollar opened, attracted by its golden bling, the Spencer name and even Russian pop stars brought in to perform there. They could take some illicit money and have it conveniently re-processed. Of course, the house took some as a commission, but they never asked any questions."

"Russian high rollers would plunk down $100,000 a visit, and receive the special treatment reserved for favoured customers, including plush hotel rooms, free food and alcohol, and chauffeur services in stretch limousines and even in helicopters."

Irina added, "Spencer considered himself immune to the law, taxation and anyone making enquiries would get lawyers buzzing around them."

Eckhart continued, "The Golden Dollar was also a place where few questions were asked. The US Treasury's Financial Crimes Enforcement Network said the casino regularly failed to report suspicious transactions or file the reports it was required to make whenever a customer gambled more than $10,000 in a twenty-four-hour period.

"This was immensely useful to Russian organised crime. Popular TV shows illustrate Atlantic City in the hands of the Mafia, but that started to decline in the 1980s. When Governor Brendan Byrne stood on the Boardwalk and warned organised crime bosses to "keep their filthy hands out of Atlantic City," there were still two Cosa Nostra gangs in residence. But the rise of gangs from Russia and South America chipped away at the Mafia dominance and the love affair between Mafia organised crime and the federal government had long since grown cold."

"Were the police on to this?" asked Christina.

"Kinda, " said Eckhart, "By 2009, the Philadelphia Police Department presented to the New Jersey Casino Control Commission showing the local branch of the Mafia was down to 20 members, from about a strength of 80 in the 1980s.

"Of those 20 members, nine were serving prison sentences, thanks to the development of new laws (especially RICO - the Racketeer Influenced and Corrupt Organizations Act), and scores of Mafia soldiers and leadership were turning state's evidence in the hope of securing lighter punishments."

Pavle continued, "It was great for Russia though, with florid scenes enacted through the Golden Dollar, thanks to its brash and rather stupid owner Logan Spencer."

"So we've got Spencer as a marked and corrupted individual now?" asked Christina.

"Yes, as you will hear, there's enough Kompromat to sink the Statue of Liberty," said Pavle.

"Tell them about Ramenkibrava," suggested Karina.

"Oh yes, organised crime...The casino became a favourite haunt of Miroslav Temirov, or 'Temi', a feared leader of the Ramenkibrava group.

The FBI believed but could never get proof that Temi was leading an international criminal organisation out of his base in Brighton Beach, dealing in drugs, extortion, and murder, and overseeing the US interests of the Ramenkibrava - that's a very tough Moscow gang.

"Agents eventually tracked Temi to a luxury condo in Spencer Tower in Manhattan, and then to the Golden Dollar, to which he made many visits under surveillance, gambling at least $250,000 there. Still nothing could be proved, either about Temi or Spencer.

"Laughably Spencer shrugged off knowing that a major Russian crime lord and money launderer was living in his own apartment block, even if he was on the floor below Spencer's own penthouse."

"It's a bit like Al Capone, isn't it?" said Clare, "Maybe the tax man cometh?"

Pavle continued, "Maybe, although the FSB were keen to nail down the Spencer affiliations now that the Golden Dollar had become such a popular spot for Russian émigrés.

"They even arranged that part of a Russian movie was filmed there: 'Deribasovskaya Darlings'. Incredibly, it was a comedy that featured a casino owned by the Russian mob. Still the stupid Spencer was unperturbed."

"This has been quite a long-term project for you?" asked Christina, "Watching the rise of one man to power?"

"Yes, but I'm not the only one who was tasked in this way. To leave Russia, many of us émigrés had to make a similar pact with the FSB to track certain individuals in the west. I just happened to have been the one that has come up trumps."

"Where does all of this lead?" asked Clare, "Are you going to do something to Spencer?"

Pavle continued, "Not exactly. We need him to know we are serious about controlling him. We will explain to him over several visits, that we have all the cards."

"That is why we have several visits ahead of us, and as part of your tour, Christina Nott."

"Yes, Tokyo, where he is in negotiations to build another casino. Los Angeles, for a meeting with three of his backers, one of whom is known personally to me, then to Seattle, to meet a fictitious high-tech backer and then to Washington D.C. to meet the man himself."

"Er - Washington?" asked Christina, "That's not on the tour?"

Irina explained, "No but by the time you've done Seattle, you'll be free of the tour and can head back via Washington."

"So, is Pavle - er Pavle are you also coming on tour with us?" asked Christina.

"No - I'm too high profile, but you will see me along the route," answered Pavle.

Bakir Jamalov

Pavle continued, "There's still more to tell...We need to explain who you will be meeting. One of the L.A. businessmen is Bakir Jamalov. He has been a construction tycoon and is a friend of mine. He was a Communist Party official born in the Soviet republic of Azerbaijan. I'll be along for the meeting with Bakir - he'll trust what we say that way."

"Bakir was chosen to set up another of the first Soviet joint ventures under the KGB for the transition to the market economy.

"That's how he was allowed by the KGB to go to the US, where he founded the US–Soviet joint venture Java Construction Industries (JCI)."

"That's how many Russians got into the USA?" asked Clare, "They were either classed as émigrés or the KGB elected them as effectively 'sleepers'?"

"That is kind of right, " answered Christina, "The KGB and FSB classified all of their agent types. There wasn't really a single 'sleeper' type agent. Instead there were a whole range of agents all with different classifications."

"Yes, and someone like Jamalov would have been put into position because he understood about business. And corrupt business practices," answered Pavle.

"Before he'd started construction in Moscow, Jamalov ran an import-export business out of a small office in midtown Manhattan and then in New Jersey.

"He was one of the agents recruited by the KGB to funnel cash into the West. In those days, any Soviet–American joint venture could be established only with KGB approval."

"So his business was being watched by the FSB right from the start?" asked Clare.

"Yes," answered Pavle, "Except at the beginning it was still the KGB - it became the FSB after the collapse of the Soviet Union. Like many joint-venture operators at that time, Jamalov and his partners started out by importing computer technology into the Soviet Union. They then expanded into trading consumer goods, including from China, into Russia, after the Soviet fall."

"Bakir Jamalov also acquired a stake in Europe's biggest outdoor market, the Cherkizon. It was claimed to be Europe's largest marketplace, located in Izmaylovo District, Moscow, Russia, near the Lokomotiv Stadium and Cherkizovskaya Moscow Metro station."

"I've even noticed that along Canal Street in Manhattan, the Chinese seem to operate their own policing," noted Clare, "The way they look at you and if they think there's a cop around they change the goods over."

"Yes, like the mysteriously disappearing Ray-Bans and Oakleys," said Christina, "But you must imagine that operating on an immense scale."

Pavle nodded, "In its heyday the Cherkizon market employed an estimated 100,000 workers, mostly Asian immigrants. It gained a reputation as the place for Chinese imports and smuggled goods, and as a 'state within a state' with its own police, customs service and courts, and many migrant workers. "

"We see it now, with the quantity of fakes that are being produced still - after many years of hunting them down," said Irina, " If you know the right places to go, right here in Saint Petersburg you can get the Fendi and Gucci fakes."

"Well," said Pavle, "Moscow city authorities closed down Cherkizovskaya in 2009 on grounds of numerous violations of regulations and illegal activities and confirmed it was to be replaced with a Chinatown. I mention it more to illustrate that Jamalov had his finger in many pies."

"This is so intertwined," said Clare, "You wonder how one man has time to get involved in so many things?"

"It's not really one man, it's the combined work of many, all of whom have allegiances to one another," said Pavle, "Be on the inside and you'll be looked after. But someone like Spencer isn't an insider and he will only experience the outside of the process."

"A case of 'done with' vs 'done to'," said Irina, "Spencer is definitely 'done to'."

Karina added, "The funds being handled by these new bankers were said by investigators to be part of the flow of Russian dirty money flooding the US since before the Soviet collapse – and much of the architecture of the transfer system appeared to be run by the KGB and the Russian mob."

Pavle continued, "Incredibly, there was no real criminal investigation, and the scheme was classified as mostly tax and customs evasion by everyday Russian business."

"I suppose it could have brought down the banking system, and a bunch of other fat cats at the time. The US Treasury and mighty US politicians didn't want that, and were slightly worried about which of their own had fingers in the pie. As a result, the KGB was omitted from allegations, as were links with US brokerages, and stock-fraud scams."

Irina chipped in, "And don't forget, another mobster, the notorious Semyon Mogilevich had long been running money into the West for the 'brava and the KGB - now there's a trail to follow!"

Christina remembered, "Semyon Mogilevich? He's the Ukranian organized crime boss, described as the "boss of bosses" of most Russian Mafia syndicates. Wasn't he put on the FBI Most Wanted list? And accused of weapons trafficking, contract murders, extortion, drug trafficking, and prostitution?"

Pavle nodded, "Oh yes, and he's had a good relationship with Vladimir Putin since the 1990s. His nicknames include "Don Semyon" and "The Brainy Don". He controls RosUkrEnergo, a company actively involved in Russia–Ukraine gas disputes, and which is a partner of Raiffeisen Bank."

Irina continued, "You'll be getting the picture by now. When Bush Senior said the 'Cold War is over,' the Russians used the perceived cooperation to deceive the US and deployed covert big guns and money to do it."

"Simply put, it meant the way was open for the Russian intelligence services and their partners in organised crime to find other ways to funnel money into the US."

"Later, a new generation of shadow bankers linked to the same mob and the KGB invented the Moldovan Laundromat for cleaning money – at least $20 billion and up to maybe $80 billion. Even later they moved into 'Londistan' and the London Laundromat, then preside dove by the very helpful blonde raggedy-haired puppet.

"But back then, one of the channels they focused on was the business operations of Logan Spencer. There was Spencer and his financial problems – it was a solution that was very much on time."

"But wouldn't Spencer see that he was being set up?" asked Clare.

Irina said, "Why should he? He was a bit stupid in any case and surrounded by rings of lawyers. Delusionally, he could think that everything he touched turned to gold, although he wasn't getting as much as the Russians."

Pavle continued, "That's right. There's no evidence that Spencer was aware there might be any issues with the former Soviet businessmen who began to line up in the early 2000s to offer him lucrative business deals. He was focused on showing what great deals he could cut. His ghost-written book around that time was called 'No such thing as too good to be true!'"

Irina said, "Spencer was still deep in debt. He'd escaped personal bankruptcy and was still wrestling with nearly $2 billion in bond debts owed by his casino and hotels group, Spencer Casino Resorts."

Pavle spoke, "Western banks had become wary of lending money to him - everyone knew that loans to him exposed the banks."

"So, Spencer could only borrow from the Russians?" asked Clare.

"More than that, Spencer was borrowing from Russian crime syndicates," answered Irina

Pavle continued, "Russia turned the lack of Spencer bank credit to its advantage. A line of former Soviet businessmen came to Spencer with proposals to build a succession of Spencer Towers. His lawyers didn't say that this was suspicious, or it got drowned out by Spencer's crowing about how much of a business genius he was."

Clare asked, "But really, he was being offered the deals that were too good to be true? He'd must have inhaled his own incense?"

"Correct," said Irina, "Now Spencer was being offered licence and management fees just for the honour of featuring his name on the buildings. His slapdash approach meant he didn't do any due diligence either. If he didn't like it later, he'd just sue instead."

Pavle added, "The businessmen who came to Spencer linked directly to the KGB or to the gang known as Ramenkibrava - The Ramenki Clan."

Irina said, "Fortunately, his own publicity machine was running full tilt during this period, and so the well-paid publicist that arranged for photographs to be taken of Spencer shaking hands with these various businessmen made a side-line offering these pictures to the FSB."

Oliver Trask

Pavle continued, "The other person we'll be meeting in L.A. is Oliver Trask. He is a Russian-American mobster, convicted felon and an ex Managing Director of Pace Investors LLC. He was caught in a stock fraud affecting the company several years ago but turned informant for the FBI.

"Ironically, he is once more involved with schemes which lead to money fraud. This time it is laundering. It is said his days are numbered if he says anything about Spencer's past, and that provides us with a unique kind of leverage over him.

When Trask first approached Logan Spencer, he had long been working with senior figures in Russian intelligence. He set up home in Brighton Beach, where Trask's father became an 'enforcer' for some of Mogilevich's interests.

Trask was brought up in a world where gangland shootings and turf wars between mafia groups were commonplace. It was also a world where Russian organised crime was expanding into white-collar crime, forging alliances with Italian crime families – first to sell bootlegged petrol, then into the diamond industry in Sierra Leone, then into stock manipulations, fraud, and elaborate commodity-trading schemes, as well as the more standard gun and drug trafficking.

Trask grew up in Brooklyn, and after starting out as a stockbroker at a series of Wall Street firms, where he ran into problems with the law. He ran a $30 million 'pump and dump' stock-fraud scheme in collusion with members of the Italian crime families, contacts he had made through his father's connections.

"What - like the Wolf of Wall Street?" asked Christina.

"Very much liked the Wolf scam. Through two New York brokerages he co-founded, Trask and his partners had secretly bought large blocks of penny stock, and then artificially inflated their price by paying off brokers to issue false statements and deploying the muscle of the Italian crime families.

"When the finance scheme collapsed in 1996, Trask left New York for Moscow, where his Brighton Beach connections helped him make friends at the top of Russian intelligence.

"Trask claimed he'd gone to Russia as a consultant for a Telecommunications company, to negotiate a $100 million deal to rent out a transatlantic cable to the United States, and that it was through this proposed deal that he came into contact with high-level officers from Russian military intelligence, who controlled Russia's telecoms.

"But he would never have gained such access so fast had it not been for his connections in Russian organised crime. Those connections included Mogilevich, who collaborated with Russian foreign intelligence.

"Then, soon after the FBI in New York uncovered a stash of documents revealing his involvement in the stock-fraud scheme, Trask contacted US intelligence officers in Moscow and offered his cooperation.

"Trask was following a time-honoured tradition. Ever since Soviet times, Russian mafia associates from Brighton Beach had offered themselves as FBI informants in exchange for criminal charges being dropped.

Christina asked, "Surely, Trask's organised-crime and Russian intelligence contacts should have set alarm bells ringing?"

Eckhart added, "You'd have thought so; It would have been impossible for Trask to gain access to such information without the active cooperation and assistance of high-ranking members of Russian intelligence and organised crime.

Pavle said, "But you have to remember, this was a world of backroom deals and a shadow economy which had operated since Soviet times. Trask knew a single misstep could land him a lifetime in jail, or more likely, pushed out of a window."

Pavle continued, "By the time Trask met Logan Spencer, he had joined forces with the Soviet trade official Ivan Maxi. Trask claimed he'd known Maxi for only three months before he agreed to go into business with him. They'd met, he said, because Maxi was his neighbour in Sands Point, an exclusive Long Island enclave, once home to William Randolph Hearst and the Guggenheims and that had been the model for The Great Gatsby's East Egg.

"Together they set up a real-estate development firm called the Salter Investments Group and moved into an office below the Spencer Organization headquarters in Spencer Tower on Fifth Avenue, staffed with beautiful eye-catching women from Eastern Europe. One of Spencer's managers started stopping by, and soon he was providing an introduction for Trask to Spencer.

Pavle continued, "The way Trask tells it, the meeting was spontaneous and on his initiative: 'I walked into his office and told him, ' I'm going to be the biggest developer in New York City.' "

Pavle continued, "Spencer laughed. I think he enjoyed Trask's picaresque approach. They started working together right away. Trask and Maxi offered Spencer a deal he could hardly refuse. The Salter Investments Group would take on the financing and construction of a series of luxury developments, paying Spencer a licence fee for the honour of using his name.

"A luxury condominium-hotel resort at Delray Beach in Florida was announced.

"There would be the $300 million Spencer International Hotel and Residence in Scottsdale, Arizona, purchased by Salter Investments at around the same time.

"Then, Salter Investments bought a site on an up-and-coming street in Manhattan's South of Houston district that would become Spencer SoHo, a $600 million forty-eight- storey luxury glass tower of condos and featuring a hotel.

"Spencer was to be given an equity stake in the project, and a steady stream of management fees, despite not having to contribute a cent.

"The deals couldn't have come at a better moment for Spencer. His poor business sense had crashed the casino and hotels branch of his empire. He was filing for Chapter 11 bankruptcy protection and another restructuring deal. He couldn't run anything except by trickery. We, the Russians, were keeping him afloat.

"The tie-up also provided potential benefits for Salter Investments. Real-estate developments offered a way around the stricter US banking regulations imposed following the Bank of New York scandal and the September 11 terror attacks."

"Didn't that slow things down?" asked Clare.

"You are right," answered Pavle, "We couldn't easily bring money in through shell companies anymore, but the money then flowed into real estate in Miami, New York and London. The shell companies and their bank accounts were all put on hold."

Karin added, "Bizarrely, real estate was exempt from any kind of reporting of suspicious activity. All of a sudden you had all these luxury condos springing up. No one asked where the money was coming from. If I'm a crook and looking around for someone to help cover things up, then the whole deal was how about I invest in your real estate."

Pavle nodded, "Yes, it became, 'I'll do the building and you provide the cover. You'll even make some money from it.' - A model for the Spencer Organization all over the world."

Then Karin said, "As late as 2018, an investigation by the US Treasury found that one in three cash buyers of high-end property were suspicious, while most sales at the top of the market took place through companies whose ownership was hidden - typically through overseas companies and trusts with offshore bank accounts. And even if those behind the schemes sold apartments at a loss they could make a profit by taking a cut for laundering the cash."

Pavle nodded, "Yes, For Salter Investment's former finance director the source of the company's funding became an alarming question. He later claimed in a racketeering lawsuit against Salter Investments that its backers included hidden interests in Russia and Kazakhstan and that the company was no more than a front for laundering cash."

Karin added, ""Tax evasion and money laundering were at the core of Salter Investment's business model and Salter Investments was largely a mob-owned and operated business which had access to cash accounts at a chromium refinery in Kazakhstan it said in a lawsuit."

Christina asked, "Presumably, Salter Investments just denied the claims?"

Pavle answered, "Yes, although Salter Investments never seemed to run out of cash. Maxi and Trask would come up with funds whenever Salter Investments was getting short of funds. Every time cash flow started getting tight, the owners would show up with a wire of funds from somewhere just large enough to keep the company going."

Clare said, "I suppose that Spencer never seemed to ask any questions"

Pavle agreed, "More than that, in court proceedings he said he never really understood who owned Salter Investments."

"Unbelievable," said Christina, "How big business works!"

Pavle continued, "Spencer began signing similar deals with a string of other former Soviet outfits. There was the half-billion-dollar Spencer Grand Ocean Resort on a stretch of prime beachfront near Miami.

"A Reuters investigation estimated that Spencer made tens of millions of dollars from the deal, in which the Soviet outfit took on all the costs and risks.

"Then for the grand-scale money laundering. A third of the over 2,000 apartments in the seven Spencer buildings had been bought through anonymous ownership vehicles - mainly LLCs - limited liability companies. A number of politically wired second- and third-tier Russian businessmen, or minigarchs, including state officials, paid out millions of dollars for condos in the Spencer developments."

"So," said Clare, "In L.A. Spencer will know Trask and know that he and Trask share certain guilty secrets."

Funnel

Irina continued, "So right now we have Spencer caught in the funnel of a trap. He is going to Tokyo to bless the construction of his new Spencer tower there, right in the middle of Minato City."

"If you don't know Tokyo so well, then Minato is a new area - like a dockland's redevelopment, right by the Tokyo Bay. Many embassies have been placed in Minato and Honda, Mitsubishi, NEC, Sony and Fujitsu all have their headquarters in that region. Google, Apple and Goldman Sachs have also moved in. It is a high prestige setting for a new tower block."

Eckhart added, "Yes but Spencer is too overextended to a agree to this contract without a new injection of funds. Some of his bonds are expiring and he has, as usual, several big repayments to make. He has already sold off one of his jewels in the crown - ironically, the Golden Dollar Casino in Atlantic City. It was found to have laundered money and a large fine was imposed, causing the casino to go into Spencer's routine Chapter 11 proceedings. In the end, it was bought by a native

American Indian tribe, who have resurrected it to a functioning building again."

Irina added, "Yes, but that is a taste of what is coming for Spencer and he must be wary of the walls closing in."

"After he thinks he's signed up for the scheme in Tokyo, we'll be visiting L.A. That's where we meet with Bakir Jamalov and Oliver Trask.

Pavle will be at the meeting and will give it the air of authenticity. The trick will be that we'll tell them that Spencer is in trouble. It should throw the cat among the pigeons."

"Spencer gets offered a deal that 'too good to be true' in Tokyo, but then has the backers rattled and pull out in L.A. Brilliant." said Christina.

"Will this be dangerous?" asked Clare, "If we start to upset powerful people?"

"Nothing worse than Christina and I are used to handling when we are on security detail," answered Irina.

"In fact, some of the stand offs will be unusual, with FSB against FSB, for example."

"Don't you have a code word or something?" asked Clare.

"No, but I think we'll be watching one another making the moves," said Christina.

Yaroslav Valerijovych Petruk

Karina continued, "The third person we will be meeting in Los Angeles is Yaroslav Valerijovych Petruk."

"Petruk became the developer for the $600 million Spencer International Hotel and Tower in Toronto, a fifty-storey block of condos and hotel rooms behind a shining glass façade.

"Spencer will also know Petruk well and if he was a rational man, he'd think he owed Petruk something for bailing him out in the past"

"Petruk was another émigré funnelling Russian wealth into bank accounts in the west. In Soviet times his father-in-law had set up a commodities trader among the first wave of financial vehicles set up by the KGB.

"Petruk had also become a key operative for the Ramenkibrava group and had close links with Salter Investments.

"Spencer was soon being courted by others who would help him expand further afield. He was approached with an offer to build the Spencer Ocean Club International Hotel and Tower in Panama.

"The planned gleaming building was to bring Spencer $70 million in fees.

"For the simple-minded Spencer, regardless of who or what was behind them, the deals looked like no-brainers. He saw them as a sign of his financial health. When the US was hurtling into the credit crunch at the end of 2007, Spencer used them as proof that his empire was firmly afloat."

"'Over a billion dollars in two prestige International developments,' he boasted to Rich Magazine, 'Why do some people say making money is so difficult?'

"The men who joined Spencer in business then were all interconnected, and by the time he was being interviewed by Rich Magazine they had taken steps to bring in more financing.

"Salter Investments continued to seek support. It signed off on a $50 million 'loan agreement' with a murky Icelandic financial company, FL Group.

"I remember FL Group, " said Christina, "They were a holding company in Iceland for two of the Icelandic airlines. Flugfélag Íslands and Loftleiðir. That's where the name came from."

Eckhart continued, "FL Group was one of a number of Icelandic banks with surprisingly deep ties to the Russian billionaire class climbing up in the wake of the dissolution of the Soviet system. The wealth of the post-USSR oligarch class was so directly tied to the Icelandic economy that astonishingly Vladimir Putin offered $5.4

billion to bail out Iceland's banks during the global financial crisis, though the deal never went through. There is still so much more untold about that story."

"FL Group structured investment as loans to avoid taxes on the dividends and called them contingent interest.

"It would otherwise be called asset stripping." said Irina, "It's a red flag that Spencer was working with these people and another red flag that they have direct links to Putin."

Irina continued, " And Christina, you'd know this, but the small size of the Icelandic economy means that most people who work in the financial sector in that country know each other.

Irina added, "Björgólfur Thor Björgólfsson, the wealthiest man in Iceland, claimed FL had been infiltrated and taken over by pro-Russian interests. He claimed it had been taken over by hostile people who were channelling Russian money through it."

"A proper local red flag, then, " said Christina, "And every Icelander knows of Bjöggi, because he was the first Icelandic billionaire! - He also asked the people of Iceland for forgiveness after the big banking crash which took down a couple of his banks in 2008."

"Yes, and that's where there is so much more to the story," said Irina.

Karina continued, "The FL Group Icelandic outfit's ownership was part of a tangled web of companies that were persistently rumoured to be connected to Putin's Kremlin, and that were soon to collapse in the financial crisis amid allegations of financial crimes.

Eckhart added, "When many of these projects went belly-up after the financial crisis, it didn't seem to matter much to any of them. First, Salter Investment's development in Delray Beach, on which more than $140 million had been spent on construction, teetered into bankruptcy.

Pavle said, "Yes, with the Delray tower still an empty concrete shell, Spencer pulled his name from the project, while Salter Investments blew dozens of buyers out of the millions of dollars they'd put down in deposits – as well as the main lender bank. And all the time Spencer was building up a big fat tax-deductible loss, as well as hiding his ill-gotten gains from non-payment to suppliers.

"The glitzy development Salter Investments had promised in Phoenix, Arizona, had never even got off the ground, locked in conflict with a local investor who alleged Oliver Trask had skimmed cash from it.

"Spencer SoHo did open with great fanfare, but Salter Investments and Spencer faced lawsuits from buyers alleging they'd been tricked into purchasing units by means of artificially inflated sales figures. Three years later, Spencer SoHo went into foreclosure.

"And four years after it opened, Petruk's Spencer Tower in Toronto was still three-quarters empty. Spencer declared it bankrupt, while the development company Petruk founded to build it had also gone bankrupt, defaulting on a $300 million loan from Raiffeisen Bank, the Austrian bank known for alleged connections with the Kremlin, and with the black-cash transfers involving Diskont Bank.

"If it was all a mirage, Spencer had still benefited hugely from licence payments and management fees, while the likes of Salter Investment and Petruk had been able to funnel money through the projects and, potentially, still make a killing.

"In a lot of places bankruptcy was very profitable. The formula was to borrow money from banks for a project and then put the project into bankruptcy. Then you walk off with the construction money. "Crash Dummy Logan" as he became known."

Plan

Clare was on the phone back to Bigsy.

"...Yeah, the band sound really good...Look, there are a few extra factors to these gigs. I think it is useful if you and Jake know. Christina won't mind me telling you."

"Er - you are in Saint Petersburg at the moment?" asked Bigsy.

"Yes, that's why I am sitting on this bench in a busy park across from the hotel."

"Ah yes, I thought I could hear traffic sounds," said Bigsy.

"I think this line will be secure," said Clare, "And I don't think anyone has followed me across the street."

"You are sounding more like Christina every day," said Bigsy, "She is leading you into strange ways. But go on tell me all about it."

'Well to start with it is no coincidence that Christina came to Saint Petersburg. It was Putin's old town, and he ruled the roost here.

"I've met a few other FSB types and they are planning a sting against Logan Spencer."

"Really? Logan Spencer! That buffoon of a man."

"Dangerous buffoon - Yes – This centres around corruption and greed," explained Clare, "They want to trap him so that he works for them."

"I thought he was supposed to be a big-shot wheeler dealer?" asked Bigsy, "Won't he spot that something is being done to him?"

"By all accounts he is a bit stupid too," announced Clare.

"Well that's what the papers have been saying for a long time," said Bigsy, "That he got a lot of his money by cheating people."

"That's right," said Clare, "He's a low level crook at heart."

"Will the band be in on this?" asked Bigsy.

"No, it will be just the Russians plus Christina and me."

"Our trip goes to Tokyo, West Coast USA and we finish up in Washington D.C."

"Wow, that's very rock 'n roll," said Bigsy.

"I think we hide in plain sight. No one political will pay too much attention to the travels of a pop band," explained Christina.

"So, Japan; don't tell me you are also working with the Yakuza?" asked Bigsy.

"You are too good, Dave Barlow," said Clare, referring to Bigsy by his real name.

Bigsy made a noise like a lorry putting on airbrakes. "'Sssssss, Phwww, you know that this could get rather dangerous?" he said to Clare.

"Yes, but Christina seems to have it under control. To be honest, I don't know how she keeps a clear head though the band gigs and then the secret agent stuff."

Clare could hear Bigsy making more noises. This time it sounded more like scraping toast.

"Are you eating?" asked Clare,

"Yes, you caught me making toast. It's toast with Marmite peanut butter on it. Best thing ever. So what else happens then? You casually meet the Japanese crime lords and...?" Clare could hear him crunching into the toast.

"Well, the Yakusa offer a dangle to Spencer. Another mega building, this time in Tokyo. Spencer will be on the hook in no time. He's characteristically short of cash and would see this new building as a massive money pot headed his way."

"I get it - you hook him with the thought of major money," said Bigsy.

"Then, when we get to L.A. We use a trio of tame Russian hoods to say that all bets are off. The Russians are known to one of the FSB operatives who we just met in Saint Petersburg. I checked him out, and he is a billionaire, so has the right credentials."

"I'm assuming he's a crooked billionaire?" asked Bigsy, "Oh yes, assume everyone from here on is a crook of some sort," said Clare, "This guy made his money from plundering Russian resources."

"That's what most of them did and are still doing," said Bigsy. "A minigarch is just a fledgling oligarch in Russia," added Bigsy.

"Yes, so we make it seem that the deal is crashed by removing the main Russian backers. They'll need some kind of 'discovery' that makes them want out."

"I see, that will weaken the proposition. No backers for the Tokyo tower means no money for the greed machine, Spencer."

"Correct, then we move to Seattle. That's where we deploy a fake technical wizard - another billionaire - who will be the potential rescuer of the deal."

"That's also where we need Spencer to do something illegal, which means we have him forever captured with his hand in the till or similar."

Bigsy said, "But Spencer isn't phased by norms of behaviour. He's said he could kill someone, and his followers would still follow him. He already abuses women if we are to believe the reports, and he certainly insults them in his political speeches."

"Yes, but we're going to do something that will damage him so deeply that he'll not recover - We're going to show that he was stealing money from the Russians to drive his political campaigns."

"Ouch, I could see how that might work. But it would need to be a lot of money and it would need to be from a high-profile person, " said Bigsy.

"Covered," said Clare, "Spencer will be implicated in a billion-dollar theft from none less than the Kremlin aka Putin himself."

"Nicely positioned," said Bigsy, "But I'd have thought this was almost impossible to pull off?"

"Watch this space," said Clare.

The Heist

"She knew all the ways of building up a mark's confidence. She knew how to feed them a little of the sweetest bait... whatever it was that they adored the most.

You were really feeding them the delicious poison of their own egos. You had to let them have a taste of it, and you had to promise them more. You had to make them believe that it would all come true."

— **Stuart Stromin, Wild Cards**

Saint Petersburg in clear

"I'm beginning to see the mist clearing around your idea," announced Christina.

Irina and Eckhart were sitting in her hotel room.

"This room will definitely be bugged," said Irina, "Look at it - it's for high rollers- the kind of people that usually get put in here will be the ones that have been invited to Saint Petersburg by friends of the system."

Christina slyly nodded, "Oh, I hadn't thought of that," she grinned winking towards Irina, "You mean to say that might overhear people in here plotting something?"

Now it was Irina's turn to grin. They could use the room to help lay the trap. A few mentions of Putin or Spencer would do it and they would set the wheels in motion.

"But, for now, let's go to the bar, shall we?"

"Great idea," said Christina. The three of them moved to leave the room.

Downstairs they were seated in around a small table in the now familiar bar. The waiter recognised Christina and asked whether she was having a good time on her visit to Saint Petersburg. Christina smiled and said it was wonderful.

Irina continued explaining the saga of Putin's rise to power.

"When Russia came out of its third revolution of the twentieth century, the Saint Petersburg sea port had a defining role to play. The Moscow kids were getting richer, but Saint Petersburg became the setting for an alliance between the KGB and organised crime that was to expand its influence across Russia, and later into Western markets and institutions too.

"This was when Vladimir Putin moved from his shadowland into the light. As the city's deputy mayor, Vladimir Putin, worked closely with the organised-crime leader who ran the port, and the oil trader who gained a monopoly on exports through its oil terminal."

"This would be like Putin practicing for how he would run Russia?" asked Christina, "Power, Money, Threats. Now we can get back to your point about Putin needing help in Saint Petersburg."

Irina said, "Let's think about him for a moment. Putin. Still young, well connected to ex-KGB, working in secret in Dresden on all manner of schemes and then transferred to Saint Petersburg, where he can't believe how awful everything is."

"Like many, he blames the Communists for wrecking everything," said Eckhart, "He's successfully burnt his past in a furnace in Dresden, so can emerge as a new animal into the streets of Saint Petersburg."

Irina added, "But Dresden taught him a few things. He's stealthy, and he understands how to make do without too many resources. A cunning man, with huge influence. He's also seen the way that the Stasi operated in Dresden and can bring some of that to Saint Petersburg. He can use state forces to corral the gangsters running black markets in the docks and cut deals with them."

Eckhart continued, "Saint Petersburg followed the same path as many other cities and began with the black marketeers, the *tsekhoviki*."

The waiter appeared and they ordered three beers.

"Craft beers?" he suggested, "We have Bakunin and Moloko?"

Christina smiled, "I'd almost forgotten about those cloudy looking craft beers here in Russia," she said, "Go on then, I'll have a Bakunin Pilsner," the other two nodded.

"Moloko? It sounds like something from Clockwork Orange," said Christina.

"Yes, Moloko+ is a beer straight out of a Kubrick movie," answered Eckhart, "But they also make more clear-looking beers nowadays - and even here in Saint Petersburg there's a few ciders."

Irina added, "So, continuing, *Perestroika* started under Andropov. But his coded message was to turn a blind eye to the black market. He knew the country was otherwise headed for mass starvation."

Eckhart nodded agreement, "Putin was well-positioned, with his KGB links. It was impossible to work in the black market without KGB connections and without protection from the KGB. Without them, no shadow business was possible."

"What had begun as corruption within the system became a KGB-cultivated testing of the future market economy, as well as a stopgap measure to fill the shortages of the command economy.

"The *tsekhoviki* black-market experiments also marked the beginning of a sudden acceleration in the transfer of the Soviet Union's vast wealth through KGB- associated friendly firms."

Irina added, darkly, "It was the wholesale looting of the Soviet state."

The waiter turned, "I hope you like these," he said, "My cousin works for Bakunin. They have grown large now and make some crazy flavoured beers." He dropped a small colourful printed leaflet onto the table. It was a Bakunin beer menu.

"Thank you, we will take a look," said Christina, as the waiter walked away.

Eckhart continued describing Saint Petersburg under Putin, "In the early nineties, the port was one of the darkest places in a city torn by gangland shootings and violent battles for cash."

Irina said, "Yes, the port was totally criminalised. There was a lot of shooting. The group who eventually took it over were part of a group of organised- crime and KGB men that came to rule the roost in St Petersburg in the nineties, and Vladimir Putin was at the centre of it.

"St Petersburg's economy was far smaller than Moscow's, the battle for cash much more vicious, and the mayor's office had tentacles extending into most businesses. The main reason for the potency of the KGB's reach in St Petersburg was that mayor Anatoly Sobchak had little interest in the day-to-day running of the city.

"He left it to Putin, who ran the foreign-relations committee, which oversaw all trade and much of the rest of the city's business, and to his other deputy who was in charge of the city's economic affairs.

"Sobchak and his deputies moved the mayor's office from the Marinsky Palace, where St Petersburg's democrat-run city council had its seat, to the warren of the Smolny Institute, from which the Communist Party had run the city since the days of Lenin's takeover.

Eckhart said, "The legacy they inherited was desperate. The city's coffers were empty. There was no cash to pay for imports, and the shop shelves were fast emptying.

"Domestic food production terrible. Grain was left to rot at the roadside by inefficient state collective farms, and bad harvests made things even worse. They not only had to deal with the food crisis, but also with an explosion of crime. In the chaos of the Soviet collapse, the institutions of power were melting away.

Irina said, "That's when the organised-crime groups moved in to fill the vacuum, running protection rackets extorting local businesses and taking over trade.

"The KGB men who took over St Petersburg with Putin were far more commercially minded than the generation that had gone before."

Eckhart nodded his agreement, "Though they mourned the collapse of the Soviet empire, many in the younger, middle echelon of the security services like Putin had quickly embraced the tenets of capitalism and rejected the dogma of the Communist Party."

"Almost ironic?" asked Christina, "to believe in something for so long and then be so quickly changed?"

Eckhart shrugged, "For this new generation, Communism had failed their empire, ruined the national economy, left them high and dry in Afghanistan and abandoned them in East Germany."

Irina continued, "Once the oil-for-food scheme was done, Putin's allies began to move in on the sea port, which initially together with the oil terminal and a fleet of ships was part of a vast state holding company known as the Leningrad Baltic Sea Fleet, or BMP. "

"I see the next move is to get embedded in the economy," said Christina.

"More than that, they could see how the systems could be corrupted to their own ends, " said Irina.

Eckhart added, "For the St Petersburg KGB men, the Baltic Sea Fleet had long been a strategic asset and the story of how Putin's people took it over is inextricably bound up with the forging of an alliance between Putin's City Hall and the city's most notorious organised-crime group, the Tambov clan.

"In its heyday, hundreds of ships had set out from Saint Petersburg (then Leningrad) carrying oil products, metals and grain, while others arrived from as far away as South America carrying fruit, sugar and smuggled goods, vital for underground operations and cash. In those days, the Baltic Sea Fleet represented the city's most strategic cash flow."

Eckhart looked around, "Most of the strength of Saint Petersburg can be attributed to its sea route access. Even in the year of the Soviet collapse its net profits were in the hundreds of millions of dollars. It was not only the owner of nearly two hundred passenger and cargo ships, it also controlled the entire Leningrad sea port, including its oil terminal, as well as the neighbouring ports in Vyborg and Kaliningrad. It was the key to the city's wealth."

Irina continued, "There's the story of how Putin and the gangsters dealt with Viktor Kharchenko. He was the man who ran the Baltic Sea Fleet at the time of Yeltsin's revolution. An avowed liberal who under Gorbachev's *perestroika* reforms had won the government's permission to carve out the company as his own fiefdom.

"Kharchenko had become increasingly independent. He was creating his separate power base just when the Saint Petersburg KGB wanted to control the cash flow.

Christina said, "So, then in the chaos of the Soviet collapse, the mobsters figured out how to exert their control?"

Irina leaned forward, "Yes - One of the first moves was made quietly. Kharchenko was returning home from a meeting with Yeltsin in Moscow when police stopped the Red Arrow train he was travelling on just outside Saint Petersburg. He was hauled off the train, charged with siphoning $37,000 out of the Baltic Sea Fleet, and jailed."

"Quite dangerous as well - being jailed like that?" asked Christina.

"Maybe they thought that killing him in prison would be too obvious. He was released on bail four months later, but by then he had been removed from his post in charge of the Baltic Sea Fleet. The Saint Petersburg KGB men installed their own director, sold off the fleet of ships one-by-one and transferred them to a myriad of offshore companies. In the process, one of the fleet's directors was shot dead.

Eckhart grimaced, "It was a raider attack. They sold off the ships for nothing. Everything disappeared. They got their way.

Irina continued, "That raid was a foretaste of operations that were to come later. The KGB men had bent St Petersburg's law enforcement to their will to take over the city's most important trading link. Now, the port and the oil terminal were being carved out from the Baltic Sea Fleet into separate entities, and privatised by Putin's City Hall."

Eckhart concluded, "Putin had arrived and installed himself, and was now protected by the Tambov Gang and the KGB. A super thug. This was an alliance between Putin, his KGB allies and organised crime that sought to run much of the city's economy for their own benefit. It's well-documented. Instead of seeking to impose order for the good of the city's population, the only order they imposed was mostly for themselves."

Irina added, "Putin seemed to be the point man providing logistical support from the mayor's office. Together with his trusted deputy Igor Sechin, he was the one who issued the licences for control of the port and the oil terminal."

"Is that THE Igor Sechin?" asked Christina, "The man who is head of Rosneft and bought Yukos?"

Irina agreed, "Yes, it's him, and he is also the leader of the Kremlin's *Siloviki* faction, a lobby gathering former security services agents in the interests of Putin. Some say he is the second most powerful man in Russia."

Eckhart continued, "The first sign of Putin's cooperation with the Tambov group came when his Foreign Relations Committee registered a Russo–German joint venture, the St Petersburg Immobilien Aktiengesellschaft, or SPAG, for investing in the city's real-estate business.

"Allegedly, SPAG laundered illicit funds for the Tambov group, as well as for a Colombian drugs cartel. Yet, during his stint as St Petersburg's deputy mayor, Putin served on SPAG's advisory board. The Kremlin said this was no more than one of many such 'honorary' positions he held as deputy mayor.

"Wow, KGB, Tambov, Columbians, this is one hell of a mix," said Christina.

Eckhart nodded, "At the start, the Tambov gang had a brutal war with the Malyshev gang right on the streets of Saint Petersburg to gain lasting and ultimate control. But after they had won it, they started fighting among themselves. An internal war developed between groups within the Tambov Gang."

Irina interjected, "Then their leader Barsukov survived a murder attempt in his car but was severely wounded and lost his arm. By then the gang had incorporated some of the racketed businesspeople and become interested in investment and fuel trading effectively evolving into a mafia."

"It is said that the Tambov Gang controls up to 100 industrial enterprises in Saint Petersburg, including PTK, the leading fuel retailer in the city, as well as four main seaports of North-western Russia: Saint Petersburg, Kaliningrad, Arkhangelsk and Murmansk."

"I knew the docks in Arkhangelsk were under gangland control when I lived there," added Christina, "Although most of the fights there seemed to be between the gangsters. Most of the time the port ran smoothly, and the regular workers had steady jobs."

"That's right," said Eckhart, "So long as they didn't notice when a drug consignment was being passed through, or some medical supplies which are really illegal munitions for Africa, for example."

Irina said, "But overall, theirs was a business that consisted of murder and raiding. The Tambov group's hands were covered in blood. There a well-known picture of Putin standing next to a jocular-looking mobster holding a sub-machine gun."

"I'm surprised those pictures were not burned as well," said Christina.

"I'm sure Putin has an eye on a furnace somewhere here in Saint Petersburg," said Irina.

Eckhart continued, "Putin's committee handed out more than $95 million in export licences to an obscure web of front companies, while virtually none of the food imports expected in return had arrived. He had special permission to award his own quotas, licences and contracts for the city's so-called oil-for-food deals, bypassing the need to agree each one with the ministry."

"Of course, Putin gave these contracts to his friends," said Irina, "And it is one of those allocations that we seek…"

Eckhardt explained, "It was also the beginning of what became a mutually beneficial alliance between the KGB and organised crime that stretched out to Switzerland, Austria and eventually to New York. A couple of these organisations were to become part of a network funnelling money from the former Soviet Union into America, including – indirectly – into the business empire of Logan Spencer.

"These organisations were also to be given access to a potentially vast source of funds, known as *безналичный*, *beznalichiye*, or 'cashless'.

"These accounting units called *beznalichiye* were distributed by state planners. Real cash was in such short supply as a result that one real rouble could be worth ten times as much as a *beznalichiye* rouble. It was a way to print money to keep the system moving.

"Soviet law forbade any enterprise from exchanging the cashless units for real cash. But under Gorbachev's reforms, some organisations were given permission to swap the *beznalichiye* for real cash simply by moving the funds from one account to another.

Irina explained, "This unlocked vast amounts of capital, and generated enormous profits."

"Then," announced Eckhart, "One of the Soviet Union's most secretive research institutes, a gigantic scientific complex deeply involved in research for laser weapons and the Star Wars race was given some *beznalichiye*."

Eckhart added, "It was part of Космические *войска России, Kosmicheskie Voyska Rossii*"

Christina asked, "The Russian Space Forces?"

"Yes, they were running the Okno observatory among other things. It's in Tajikistan since the USSR was divided," replied Eckhart, "Its head originally granted the team access to 170,000 roubles in *beznalichiye*, worth nearly two million roubles in real cash. He didn't even ask what they would do with the money.

"I see, there's been so much unaccounted cash sloshing around in the ex-Soviet system, that some of it must still be sitting in undiscovered accounts," ventured Christina.

"Well, it's that Space Force transaction that gives us our best lead," answered Irina.

Rehearsal 3

Christina had already realised by the third rehearsal that Jallie T's band were great musicians. They could play anything, and it sounded like the way she had originally intended it to be played.

Their keyboard player Ellie was great with samplers too and they had downloaded Christina's samples library to use as part of some of the tracks.

They had all the special software too: Ableton Live, MainStage and a couple of Macs to help drive the technical side of things. Christina couldn't think of another band that she'd played with that had so much technical know-how as well as musicianship.

Jallie T herself was used to composing on a Mac, Ellie played keys and used software samples and even Lucas in the control room was all over the technical side of things, including DMX-ing the lights.

They'd played through most of Singularity by now, including;

- My body
- Wind
- Rain
- Hey DJ
- Your eyes
- Long way down
- Earth
- Tell me what you want from me
- Feel your body all over mine
- Remember me
- Splitting the diamond
- I'm your hit man, babe

These, (except for the complex splitting the diamond) were all performance ready.

It still left a few more songs that Christina had written, performed, but never recorded.

"Some of these are the more autobiographical ones, " she explained, "Lets see now:

- **No more moon-base alpha:** that's the where the nearest available instrument was a banjo, and the song is designed to be an artefact from the near future. I'd prefer it to have clicks and scratches actually.

- **Triple A rated (hot air):** A political song.

- **E.S.T (Electro Shock Therapy):** I need to break this habit. Bad songwriting. I'm getting jitters. Yesterday, I wrote the song on my iPhone, whilst in bed after an oval-tabled dinner with a few friends. Tonight, I was supposed to be at another dinner, but it was cancelled, so I headed home and watched a couple of episodes of the excellent and twisty supernatural 'Being Human'. I was doing fine for two episodes, but to avoid getting sucked into the next one I had to resist the brilliant trailer. The storyline had a gothic edge and plenty of hospital scenes. Before I could stop myself, my next ten-minute cascade of ill-formed words were dripping from my fingers.

- **French kiss-off:** I thought it would be better to move the action to a little town in France, and have a proper silent bust-up, where she just leaves in her little Citroen without any explanation.

- **One card at a time:** deal a card my sister.

- **La dama puliendo el pastor todo la calle reale:** The last time I was in Mexico.

- **You can be my vampire if I can be your werewolf:** Written during a trip to Brussels.

- **Motorway adventures in Wales:** Parisian conference call and a trip to a motorway hotel. Oh, the glamour.

- **American Automobile (gotta get an):** I saw Cadillac Ranch off Route 66 in its grey era, when it looked like Stonehenge.

- **Vladless:** about a film camera missing in action.

- **Dreaming with Galina:** Name changed to protect the guilty.

- **Some of your stuff ain't normal:** Not sayin' its the vodka in the fridge,' those bottles full a' broken glass. Not sayin' its the way you shake your skin. But some of ya, some of ya, some of ya stuff ain't normal

- **Model romance (je t'aime):** Actually written in Barcelona, with my lovely French lady of dreams.

- **Prophesy:** Love the guitar twiddles in this one. They are like sparkling earworms.

Christina continued, "I know it's a lot, but I doubt if we'd need more than a couple to play as extra stand-by tunes. Oh yes, and 'Crash' - the one we play if the computers go down or something crazy happens on-stage."

After band practice on the fourth session, Jallie T suggested that everyone head out for the evening into the main part of Saint Petersburg.

"We are doing so well, let's celebrate," she said. The others did not need any encouragement, and they were soon in the bright lights part of the city.

"Look - a Casino!" said Alex, as they all looked across the street.

Christina's alarm bells were ringing. The venue screamed 'organised crime' and 'tourist trap' both at the same time.

"Okay, then," she said, as they crossed the street and entered via an opulent lobby. She looked across at Clare, who was similarly giving off 'don't touch anything' signals.

"This is very fancy," said Clare, "But I wonder how they afford everything,"

"Look - That's where you get gaming chips and plastic, " said Nate, he and the other members of the band hurried over to the cashier area.

"They'll want passports as part of ID checks," said Christina.

Sure enough, Ellie and Raff returned crestfallen that they were unable to play. "You'll be able to go on some of those slot machines, I expect," said Clare, pointing to the flashing lights."

They both cheered up at the thought of this and moved towards the commotion.

"I've been on so many missions with high-rollers who want to visit casinos, that I am unaffected by it all now," said Christina.

"Me too," said Clare, "I visited Vegas a couple of times, but I was more into the shows than the gambling part. Unless you've a small fortune it can all be rather tacky."

"Yes, and the entire place is wired too, so you'll be on camera in here everywhere, including the restrooms and the elevators."

"Yes, in Vegas the elevators had slots in them as well," said Clare,

"If you look over there, they have them here too," observed Christina.

"I think we might need to babysit the boys," said Clare, "Look they have just gone into that area with the poles."

"They're having a good time; don't let us spoil it," said Christina, "Wait, here comes one of the dancing girls, let's watch their reaction!"

An impossibly flexible woman in a leotard had just appeared and was swinging around on a shiny pole set in the middle of the gambling machines. A similarly dressed woman was walking along with a mirrored tray of free cocktails, tastefully served in plastic beakers.

Clare and Christina looked at one another and burst out laughing.

Putin's casino

The next morning Christina, Eckhart and Irina were eating breakfast in the hotel.

"I hear you were out on the town last night!" said Irina.

"That's right, the band decided to hit the bright lights and ended up in one of the Casinos."

"Which one was it?"

"I think it was called the Admiral - or something like that."

"The Admiral, that's one of the first casinos, and one that Vladimir Putin had a direct interest in! It's changed its name several times since he had an interest there, but it is still fundamentally the same place."

"Let's not forget that Vladimir Putin was St Petersburg's chairman of the supervisory board for casinos and gambling.

"He began issuing gambling licenses in which shares were gained by the city of St Petersburg in the company

Neva Chance which owned the first St Petersburg casino AOZT Casino. Originally it even had the same address and phone numbers as city hall.

Later it became JV Casino Neva СП «Казино Нева») Then it changed its name to Laguna, followed by Admiral Club or more simply known as Admiral.

Eckhart added, "To mix things up further, a Yakuza boss Kinichi Kamiyasu supplied slot machines with cash prizes to St Petersburg casinos in the 1990s from his Stockholm, Sweden, company Dyna Computer Service AB."

Irina added, "Yes, The Yakuza and the local Russian mobsters set up a joint venture JV Petrodin (*СП «Петродин»*)

"The company JV Petrodin, was 35% Kamiyasu/Yakuza owned and two local Russian mobsters owned the rest through their company BXM (*БХМ*). They used the money from the casinos to provide capital for Bank Rossiya."

"What? Putin's Bank?" asked Christina.

Eckhart added, "Nowadays the Kremlin denies that Mr Putin has any links with Bank Rossiya.

"The reason this financial institution is perceived as linked to Mr Putin lies in the long history its backers have with the president, and the fact that the bank rapidly gained access to some of the Russian state's most prized assets after Mr Putin took power in Moscow. Putin even involved himself in co-ownership of a luxury dacha complex with some of these backers. One can see why some describe the bank as a 'special purposes vehicle' for a closed group of people.

"Putin would deny any involvement, though, wouldn't he?" asked Christina.

Irina asked Christina, "You can start to see how things are coalescing around KoKo and its vast collection of anonymous offshore companies, ex KGB secrets, the Bank Rossiya and some of the wastage from the frantically busy neo-oligarchs?"

Christina nodded.

Irina added, "Add in that the Yakuza feel as if they were left out in the cold when all the Russian moguls and money moved into the Bank. They are someone else we will visit in Tokyo."

Christina smiled, "So we have FSB/KGB secrets, KoKo, secret offshore companies, dubious banking, mobsters, black markets, Bank Rossiya, mad young oligarchs and Yakuza. And forgive me...that's not even our top mission?"

PART TWO

Trigger

"The best ideas will eat at you for days,
maybe even weeks,
until something,
some incident,
some impulse,
triggers you to finally express them."

— Criss Jami,

Friday flyway

I can't believe its Friday come around already!" said Christina.

Yes, said Irina, "We'll be in Japan by Sunday!"

"Well, I think we've got the music covered off, but as for the other two plans...

   1) Logan Spencer and
   2) The Moneytree...aka Denis.

I think both of them need more work. I feel I now know more about how we are going to work Logan but have very little idea about the other."

"You must forgive us, said Irina, "Eckhart and I have been planning the other opportunity for a long time. We are still cautious to tell others about it. For example, it could leak to people who could turn the tables on us."

"I understand that, " said Christina, "But if we are all to work together on this, then you will need to fully trust me."

"Okay, I'll explain more on the flight, let's be sure to sit together."

They were travelling with Lufthansa, flying first to Frankfurt for a seven-hour stopover and then travelling on to Tokyo Haneda.

They met the rest of the band at the check-in. They had been busy checking through flight cases with guitars and equipment. Eckhart had travelled with the band and was supervising the loading of the equipment.

"It'll be fine," he said, "and with Lufthansa you can be sure it will get to the other end."

"We've hired most of the gear at the venues," said Lucas, "Drums, cabinets, amps, lighting rig. It is so much simpler and so much less stuff to worry about. We've a few guitars, a couple of keyboards - one of which is a Virus so we could easily get a replacement, plus the Macs, some microphones and everyone's ears. Oh yes, and a whole box full of pedals, launchers and effects. Thanks to Eckhart, I gave him the specs and he's sent on ahead for it."

"Launchers?" asked Clare, "are you intending to shell the crowd?"

"No, they are the button packs that we use to trigger some of the sounds," answered Lucas.

"You know," said Jallie T, "I think, Christina, you are better funded than Erebus, the band we are supporting! Have you got a secret financier or something?"

"Very secret," answered Christina, "They really do want this to be a successful mission."

"Mission, I like it," nodded Nate, "Sounds very cool,"

Christina noticed that Nate and Ellie seemed close and that they were melting deliberately into the background, "We'll see you airside at the gate," said Ellie, "and don't worry we'll be there."

Lucas nodded, "Great, I've got all the instrument passports and stuff, make sure you refer anything about the kit to me."

They nodded and walked away holding hands.

"Together?" asked Christina, "Yes, it must be two or three years by now," said Lucas. Christina could see he was still in 'sheepdog mode' counting everything and everyone. She backed away.

"Okay, I'm heading through security to get airside," announced Christina.

"I'll come too," said Irina. Eckhart nodded as if to follow and then Alex skipped over, "Good plan, and there're more facilities on the inside."

"*Dasvidaniya, Russia,*" said Christina. Irina and Eckhart nodded, and they all walked towards the border controls.

Business Class

Christina and Irina were sitting next to one another in Lufthansa Business Class. The rest of the band were sprinkled around other Business seats and by their whoops of pleasure Christina decided that they felt pleased to be travelling with so much leg room.

Clare had settled next to Nate the lead guitarist and Ellie and Raff were in a couple of seats at the back of the section. Lucas was in middle row, chatting to a business woman who looked as if she was trying to get some work done on a laptop.

"Okay Irina, it's time for you to explain more of the other scheme...I have a thought that the two plans are somehow interlinked? - Maybe we are going to frame Logan Spencer with the stolen money?" asked Christina.

"Yes, you are right!" exclaimed Irina, "That way we stay in the clear and Spencer gets the blame."

"I knew it," said Christina, "This really is a once in a lifetime opportunity for you!"

"For us," corrected Irina, "We meant what we said about you being a 1/3 partner for this."

The pilot interrupted with some comforting words about the flight. The air stewards performed their ballet explaining how the emergency procedures operated.

Irina added, "So to recap. Putin moved into Saint Petersburg, set up some rackets with the local mobsters and uses a variety of financial means to multiply and then salt away the money. You'll find the stories in The New York Times just as much as in the memories of Saint Petersburg residents. No one dared to oppose him, because he had protection from both the KGB and the local Tambov gang, who are like Russian mafia.

"Most of Putin's deals were with his friends, many of who he made in Dresden when the KGB could operate there in darkness.

Occasionally there would be a deal that was away from his friends and comrades, and one such deal was to the Russian Space Forces, where his people were multiplying money by ten or twenty, using *beznalichiye,* i.e. cashless money to drive up his profits.

"Then he used casinos (like the one you visited) and banks (like the speculated Rossiya Bank) to operate his money laundering. That's a move from the small-scale of black-markets to the big-time of laundering the cashflows of the ascendant oligarchs. Along the way, he and his mobster friends find a few foolish foreign businessmen whose greed drives their business sense. One of them is Logan Spencer, who becomes a high-end laundromat, specialising in cash for property and cash for projects.

"Perfect so far, but we need to find the chink in the armour," said Christina.

"It's not so much a chink as a portal," answered Irina, "Remember they made a play for the port of Saint Petersburg and the oil terminal? - When the mobsters sold off all of the ships?"

"Yes," answered Christina.

"Well they didn't realise what a good thing they were on to," answered Irina, "The mobsters had seen the port through their own eyes, as the place they could import black market goods and export illicit items such as guns.

"It didn't take them long to realise, even after they had sold off the ships, that Saint Petersburg was a real money-making machine. It carried most of Russia's oil through the terminals, allowing wholesale skimming and there was always a supply of inbound cocaine which could keep most of Russia and Europe high. At one stage they even took in some counterfeit money from the Camorra. Unbelievably, the Italian gangs had beached $1 bills and then overprinted them as $100s for distribution around Russia.

"So let's take a quick look at that oil terminal... Gennady Timchenko, was ex-KGB and had known Putin since their days studying spy craft together at the Red Banner Academy.

"Does this provide a direct link from Putin's KGB buddies to Saint Petersburg rackets?" asked Christina.

"You work it out, they were even judo buddies," said Irina. She paused and looked out of the window of the plane. It was positioned on the runway and started its acceleration towards takeoff. They halted their conversation as they listened to the judder of the plane bouncing along the runway. A little more noise from the engines and they were up in the air. A short time later there was a clonk sound as the wheels retracted.

Irina continued, "Timchenko wanted the Saint Petersburg oil terminal and Kirishineftekhimexport set up as an oil trader. Rumours were that it was one of those friendly firms used to transfer Communist assets but Timchenko denied it. Now, even with his connections, Timchenko was unable to gain access to the St Petersburg oil terminal.

"Remember Kharchenko? - The guy that they had to lock up to wrest control away?", asked Irina.

Christina nodded.

Irina continued, "At that time, not only was the oil terminal part of Kharchenko's fiefdom, but as the power of the Soviet Union fractured, it became a battleground for the city's warring criminal groups. Gaining control of exports through the St Petersburg terminal was so important that Timchenko turned to City Hall for assistance."

"I see, we get a direct documentable link - it is the first one, I think," said Christina.

"Yes, Timchenko set up a joint venture with Putin's Foreign Relations Committee called 'Golden Gates'. They aimed to bypass the existing terminal and raise Western financing to build a new, upgraded terminal.

"This was the first time the ties between Putin and Timchenko had emerged into the open. But the arrangement fell apart when one of the chief negotiators died suddenly, with whispered rumours of poisoning."

"There's an awful lot of mystery deaths and suicides around this story," observed Cristina.

Irina added, "Yes, then another member of the Golden Gates group, Sergei Shutov, was threatened and told to stay away from the project. The project was under severe attack, with St Petersburg's mafia groups, including the Tambov, battling each other to gain control of revenues from the existing terminal.

"The Tambovskaya Bratva were playing hardball. The pressure mounted to such a degree that Putin sent his two young daughters away to Germany for their safety."

"They must have all seen the money in the terminal?" asked Christina.

"You know, I don't think they did. I think the only person who realised the run-rate through the terminal was Timchenko," answered Irina.

"Anyway, eventually, a deal was struck with hardcore mobster Ilya Traber fronting the seaport and an agreement that Timchenko could move his oil through the port. But if you need to ship oil through a port full of bandits, then you need agreements."

"Otherwise it's just getting robbed continuously by the mobsters. I had to run security for some similar talks between mobsters and businesses," said Christina.

Irina nodded, "This is where Timchenko could draw on his network of KGB-linked foreign bankers to finance his trading operations. They had links with Dresdner Bank and some of Putin's old buddies. Nowadays Timchenko is head of Gunvor Group and Forbes reckons he is worth around $15 billion. You see the kind of sums in play?"

Irina smiled as she thought about it, "Ilya Traber was an old school henchman from mobster central casting who used to intimidate bankers by bringing them from Pulkovo airport to his high gated compound in an armoured car. There he would sit, in tracksuit bottoms and wearing enormous gold jewellery, like he'd watched one too many Bond villains at work."

"Does this imply a deal where Putin has helped set up the oil terminal?"

"That's what it looks like, and then it sees so much money flow through it that no-one knows what to do with it all."

"Ahah, so a new banking instrument is needed to put the money somewhere?"

"Precisely. And that's where the *beznalichiye* scheme comes in. As long as there was a regular income to the *beznalichiye* accounts, then it could easily be converted to USD hard currency at a 10 to 1 rate. And so suddenly, all of that skimmed oil and cocaine money becomes legitimate!"

Right, so we have a trail, and an ever-increasing stack of money. How do we get to access it then?

"Whose account was it in? The Russian Space Agency. That famous money-eating project that died a death along with America's Star Wars."

"I don't think that is strictly true though, is it?" asked Christina, "I even bought a ROSCOSMOS tee- shirt in that souvenir shop outside the rehearsal studio."

"No, you are correct, but think carefully, the Space Agency was without true leadership in its early years. Control was spread through many departments resulting in turf wars.

"Its history is choppy - for something as significant to Russia as NASA is to America,"

Irina looked at her notes:

- **1992: Russian Space Agency** (Российское космическое агентство, *Rossiyskoye kosmicheskoye agentstvo*), or RKA

- **1999: Russian Aviation and Space Agency** (Российское авиационно-космическое агентство, *Rossiyskoye aviatsionno-kosmicheskoye agentstvo*), commonly known as *Rosaviakosmos* (Росавиакосмос),

- **2004 : Federal Space Agency (Roscosmos)** (Федеральное космическое агентство (Роскосмос), *Federalnoye kosmicheskoye agentstvo (Roskosmos)*),

- **2015: the Federal Space Agency (Roscosmos)** was abolished and the Roscosmos State Corporation for Space Activities was established by a presidential decree.

"It claimed it was short of cash into the early 2000s, and only when it was pulled together and the Duma gave it a serious budget (some 305 billion roubles or US$11 billion) did things really move forward."

Christina grinned, "I see, the diffused responsibilities meant that accounts were not being monitored? The Agency thought it was broke, but a strange and illegal cashflow was heading in from the Saint Petersburg oil terminal."

Irina nodded, "That's right. This would be one of several places that the oil terminal would have spread its money, over many years."

"But won't it have gangster fingerprints all over it? And worryingly what about the FSB?"

"That's just it. We think it has been forgotten. With the transfers of people out of Traber's business, Timchenko moving on to bigger things and the various assassinations in the Tambovskaya Bratva, we think that no-one is left who will remember the specific accounts."

"Okay, but so how do we find the right account? And then how do we move the money out?"

At that moment the air-steward arrived, "Here is your menu, would you like to choose some food and maybe a lovely German wine?"

Putin's dacha

They poured their wine and quietly ate their airline meals.

"Schnitzel mit Nüdeln," said Christina, "These are few of my favourite things!"

"Yes and Apfelstrüdel to follow. Someone is having some fun," said Irina, "...Something else I guess you didn't know about Putin was that he has property interests?"

Christina looked surprised, "That's quite capitalist, isn't it?" she asked,

"Yes, Putin organised the building of a group of dachas."

"Ah yes, the Soviet people always have a dream to have a dacha, " said Christina.

"But also the understanding that it was necessary to have the right neighbours. Putin chose a piece of land north from Saint Petersburg through the forests and lakes of Karelia.

"Near the border with Finland, is Komsomolskoye Lake, renowned for its excellent fishing. Before Putin moved in, the road had been no more than a dirt track. But soon after the new inhabitants arrived it was asphalted over, and lights were installed.

"You'll have seen those bare-chested pictures of Putin fishing and horse riding? They were taken out by his dacha."

"Oh yes, the cami-fatigues! I think they even made a calendar! And several viral Photoshopped images!"

Christina laughed, then whispered, "I'm so glad we are on Lufthansa, you know, I'd worry on Aeroflot about giggling about *botoksnyj (ботоксный)*."

"Ha Christina - *botoksnyj* - botox face - I can tell you have lived abroad. Most of us here still say Мистер Пу (Mister Pu) or *старик Кабаев (the old man Kabaev)*- since his association with Alina Kabaeva - that 30-year younger Russian gymnast."

"And wasn't the paper that revealed his relationship to her shut down?" asked Christina.

"Yes, you don't mess with Mister Pu!" said Irina, "But back to Lake Komsomolskoye. The villagers who'd lived for generations on the lakeshore saw new, more powerful electricity lines installed, though none of the power reached their homes.

"Instead they were asked, one by one, to move away, and were either given money to leave or provided with new ready- built houses further inland. Their new neighbours built imposing Finnish-style chalets on vast tracts of land.

"The Putinites formed a group that became known as the дачный потребительский кооператив «Озеро» - The Ozero Dacha Cooperative. They took over the lakeshore, from which their former neighbours were cut off by a high new fence.

"The men who moved to Lake Komsomolskoye with Putin were the blue blood of his KGB acquaintances. Mostly shareholders of Bank Rossiya, they had been connected to Putin since even before the Saint Petersburg days.

After Putin became president, he and his allies from the Ozero dachas began to capture strategic sectors of the economy, creating a tight-knit network of loyal lieutenants – trusted custodians – who took control of the country's biggest cash flows and excluded everyone else."

"This would include the people he'd made as friends and trusted allies from his days in Dresden?" asked Christina.

"That's right, and other colleagues from the KGB Red Banner Academy in Moscow," answered Irina. "Bank Rossiya was to form the core of the financial empire behind this group, and it was to spread its tentacles throughout Russia, and deep into the West too."

"But he'd still need a trusted banker for all of this to work?" asked Christina.

Irina nodded, "That's right; one of the new near neighbours was a banker for Rossiya bank. Filippov Vladimir (Vova) Zakharovich.

"He had a job to set up suspense accounts to manage the temporary burst of money from the various illegal schemes. It was like a 'holding tank' to put the money into before it was allocated to a legitimate sounding business.

Come to think of it 'holding tank' sounds too small for the money involved. Warehouse would be a better description.

This money was undetectable until it landed 'purified' somewhere else.

"Well, the Press got interested. A couple of searches took place. One was through the well-known Paradise Papers. You may remember them. A huge discovery of financial transactions, including those of Her Royal Majesty Queen Elizabeth II. The expose was unremarkable in headline terms. No one could be found to have done anything particularly illegal. Morally dubious sometimes, but all within the law.

"But it did highlight a something relevant to us though. The use of an intangible asset against which to store money. Instead of, say, putting the money into real estate, it could be stored against a valued trade secret or patent.

Christina could see that Irina was looking through her small notebook again.

"Computer firm Apple did plenty of this in Ireland. A great deal of Apple's intangible property was exposed around the time of an internal Apple Inc. reorganization of three Irish subsidiaries.

It meant in 2015 Apple's gross domestic product showed a sudden 26% increase, and around $270 billion of intangible assets suddenly appeared in Ireland as the year began – more than the entire value of all residential property in Ireland. Apple might have taken advantage of a tax incentive known as a capital allowance, which gives Irish companies generous tax breaks for buying intangible property – essentially intellectual property like patents.

"In other words, Apple allegedly transferred them from Bermuda to a subsidiary located in Ireland for the tax incentives and didn't have to pay any tax on the intra-company transaction in Bermuda either.

"Now that is all water under the bridge for Apple. They were at one time expected to pay Ireland an $11-billion tax bill, which was still relatively small compared to the money they were moving around, but that was quashed in July 2020. Like all good shell games, the Intellectual Property has moved to Jersey now.

Hold that thought though; another type of organisation that has a lot of Intellectual Property is - Yes - A Space Programme.

"Ahah, like the one that had been loaned the money?"

"Yes, the very same. Let's take look at a different leak of banking information. This time, the more headline grabbing Panama Papers. Remember those? That's when the shady lawyers Mossack Fonseca operated out of Panama and set up around 214,000 shell companies, from a small office block in Panama City?

"Many of the small companies were allegedly to assist with money laundering through the property markets. Aside from a few well-known politician and celebrity names, that became the main story.

"A favoured shell company investment is real estate in Europe and North America. London, Miami, New York, Paris, Vancouver and San Francisco have all been affected. The practice of storing assets in luxury real estate has been frequently cited as fuelling skyrocketing housing prices .

"There is a huge amount of dirty money flowing into Miami that's disguised as investment. In Miami, three quarters of condo owners pay cash, a practice considered a red flag for money-laundering.

It is similar in London. Real estate in London is frequently purchased by overseas investors. Britain's National Crime Agency, said that "the London property market has been skewed by laundered money. Prices are being artificially driven up by overseas criminals who want to sequester their assets here in the UK".

As well as corporations, there was a group of headline grabbing personalities allegedly involved as well, including government officials like, "

Irina referred again to her small notebook,

"This is all in the Panama Papers expose:

"Here we are: Michael Ashcroft, retired Member of the House of Lords; Tony Baldry, former Member of the House of Commons; David Davies, former Chief Scientific Adviser to the Ministry of Defence; Michael Mates, former Member of the House of Commons; and Pamela Sharples, Member of the House of Lords."

Irina flipped a page.

"And linked with government officials were: Sarah, Duchess of York, former wife of Prince Andrew; Ian Cameron, father of Prime Minister David Cameron; David Sharples, son of Baroness Pamela Sharples; Mark Thatcher, son of former Prime Minister Margaret Thatcher."

She looked across to Christina.

"Add to that a couple of dozen footballers, people like Aaron Banks (the Brexit tycoon) and Simon Cowell (the TV games show maker), and there's quite a list beginning to form. Of course, while the news was still hot it was burning up the media, but then something else came along to swamp it and everyone moved away from looking at it. "

"Now we took more of a deep dive into the names. Guess who we found, linked to five separate nondescript companies?

"Someone with Saint Petersburg connections?" asked Christina.

" Oh yes, none other than Putin's close neighbour at the dacha, Filippov Vladimir Zakharovich. You remember, the banker from Rossiya Bank?"

"Oh yes, of course, Putin's neighbour and a banking official!"

"Well, Vova had been busy. He'd used several of the Delaware shell companies formed by Kaveladze and then linked in some companies in Panama. It was clever, because it hid the flows of money.

These money flows seemed to have the express purpose of taking the suspense account money from Rossiya Bank and allocating it into a little range of businesses. It was done deftly, with random smaller amounts showing each small business to be making a healthy but non-taxable turnover."

"Kaveladze had used the Russian Space Program Projects as the basis for allocating Intellectual Property among the companies, which all had some links to space exploration.

- двигательные установки ограничены - DUO Booster Rockets
- пусковые системы россии - PSR Launch Systems
- невесомые грузовые лебедки - HGL Weightless Cargo Winches
- космические навигационные системы - KNS Cosmic Navigation Systems
- Средства защиты дикой природы - SZDP Wildlife Protection Frames

Christina laughed as she heard the company names. "It all sounds so plausible, except the last one? - Were they expecting to catch an Alien or something? - To put its mouth dripping horror into a cage?"

"Stranger things have happened. They took some geckos into space to see how they would get along; it ended in tears though," answered Irina.

"You know, I'd be more worried if there were alien geckos back on earth. Return of the giant lizards!" said Christina.

"Well the upshot of all of this is that Kaveladze set up a nice little range of businesses, off-shore and undetectable, to receive the older run-rate of funds from the Space Project, paid in by the deft banker Vova Zakharovich.

However, it could be said Vova Zakharovich was found out by the Panama Papers investigation.

"Lucky his name started with a Z - the last to be investigated," laughed Christina.

"Well, remember I've told you about the mysterious deaths...A couple of things happened, Zakharovich was stricken with a virus which attacked his central nervous system. He went into a coma but never recovered and died in hospital.

About the same time, his dacha and that of Putin were both caught in a mysterious fire and burnt to the ground. Putin said he escaped from the sauna in his dacha with just a towel. I guess Zacharovich's dacha was empty."

"Zacharovich must have annoyed someone?" guessed Christina.

"Plainly - someone was hiding the evidence and taking no chances that Zacharovich had more hidden away in his dacha," answered Irina,

"But it does have the side effect that there is now no-one who knows about the missing money or the five special companies that were set up to sweep the money away."

"And Putin covered his tracks by his own dacha also going up in flames?" asked Christina.

"That's right, although you'd hardy know that now, Putin had his rebuilt to a grander specification.

"So Zacharovich's secrets were buried along with him?" asked Christina.

"That's what we think and those secrets are what we are going after," said Irina.

Christina realised that Irina was finally starting to trust her.

Follow Me

*"follow the money and follow the troops,
don't follow the tweets"*

former CIA Director
General David Petraeus

Follow the Money

"So does that lead us to where the money is stashed?" asked Christina.

We've got the companies and we know their bankers, from the Panama Papers, answered Irina.

"It looks as if Zakharovich was playing it safe when he moved the money around. He moved it to a German bank. Deutsche Union Bank (Dresden). Now a little known fact about German Banking is that they still support Bearer Bonds."

"I thought they had been phased out? Asked Christina, "I thought that Switzerland and Luxembourg were among the last to go?"

"Not exactly, the Germans are surprisingly non-compliant according to Transparency International - They only fully support one of the twenty G20 Principles. Everyone just assumes that Germany will do everything by the Regeln."

"I've heard of people using these kind of bearer schemes before, but not on this scale," said Christina.

"It is still a weapon of choice amongst money launderers. Get the money made clean, extract it in one jurisdiction and then pay it back in another, a small amount at a time. You'll have heard the drug cartels do something similar?"

"Okay, but how would we gain access in the first place?"

"That's the power of the FSB. For this mission I had a couple of extra passports and back stories made up, for each of us actually, although I don't think you'd need it Christina."

"I've got a Canadian Passport and a German one, and Eckhart has an additional Russian passport and a German one."

"You didn't?" asked Christina, half guessing what Irina had done.

"Yes, I arranged for Eckhart's Passports to have the name 'Filippov Vladimir Zakharovich.'"

"That's brilliant, so Eckhart can visit Deutsche Union Bank with either a German or Russian passport in the name of Zakharovich?"

"Correct, and he can that way arrange for money to be either transferred or, worst case, for us to get bearer bonds."

"I assume it would it be better for the money to be transferred rather than having the bonds issued?"

"Yes, but we'll need a plausible company to move it to, one that is used to paying and receiving large sums."

"We'd need something that looked realistic, with a big website and all, that's where we fall down in the current plan and why we'd need to take paper bonds."

Christina thought for a moment, "I think I might have someone that can help us," she said, "via Clare."

There was a gentle sound in the cabin. One of the Lufthansa crew walked through.

"Ladies and gentlemen, if you would be so kind as to check that all of your seatbelts are fastened. The Captain informs that we are about to go into an area of mild turbulence. Thank you."

"Mild turbulence," thought Christina, "An understatement if ever I heard one."

Frankfurt Flughafen

They were all in the airport. "We've some rooms booked for the stay here, on the airport, in the hotel complex called 'The Squaire', said Eckhart, "We've got a day rate, shared doubles, but it means we can all freshen up."

"I like this travelling with you, Christina Nott," said Jallie T, "and you'll be pleased to know the whole band approves too. Business class and layover hotel rooms is pretty cool."

"Well, that means we'll be rested and relaxed by the time we reach Tokyo," said Christina, "The second flight is longer than that one,"

"I couldn't get Business Class on the next leg," said Eckhart smiling, " We've had to travel First Class instead."

"Show me to the lounge," said Raff,

"Not until we've seen these hotel rooms," giggled Ellie.

"I'll go with Clare," said Christina. The others quickly paired up and Irina was to share with Eckhart.

Jallie T had a room to herself.

"Its further from here to Tokyo than it is from Vancouver," said Alex.

"One more sleep until you see Erebus again!" said Nate.

Everyone headed for the hotel, which was a sleek modern building, clearly part of a newer terminal complex, it looked as if they were still building some parts of the terminal.

Christina mused that airports never looked finished, there was always some part of it being rebuilt or extended.

Then Clare and Christina found their room. Two double beds and a beige decor.

"This is done out in German beige. They have used this colour scheme forever," said Christina. They both looked slightly aghast at the swirly carpet.

"It looks like someone has dragged tree trunks through sand," said Clare, "But hey there's lots bottles of goodness in the bathroom,"

"That pandemic certainly brought back the individual shampoos and other nice things," said Christina, "Remember when hotels were quietly bolting big bottles to the walls?"

Clare nodded.

"So what did you find out from Irina?" asked Clare, "do you know any more about either the mission or the 'other mission'?"

"So much to tell and I think we might have something for Bigsy," answered Christina.

"In order to frame Logan Spencer, they want to show that he has swindled some money. I think they want the money to lead back to Putin. Imagine that. There will be no return for Spencer."

"He's already in up to his neck isn't he? Didn't the Russians bale him out by giving him lots of 'laundromat' money?" asked Clare.

"Well, that's what some of the news is saying, but Spencer says it is all Fake News, of course."

"So how will it work?" asked Clare.

"Well they have found out where a lot of money has been stored," explained Christina.

"It was originally fed into a Russian Space Program organisation, but then it was hidden away in a group of offshore companies.

"A devious banker named Zakharovich moved the money to a set of bank accounts in Germany. We can access the German accounts, but it requires Eckhart to pose as Zakharovich. He's even got an FSB-provided fake passport."

"Okay - that all sounds complicated, but why is Bigsy needed?"

"Well, to do the other part of the mission - in effect to set up Spencer, someone needs to pose as CEO of an American Space Company. That way, the American company can take the payments from the German bank accounts without arousing suspicion. The five companies involved are all related to space in some way or another."

"I see, Eckhart is going to get the money moved to the new accounts. Became they look like business payments it will get around Anti Money Laundering legislation."

"Yes, and Germany isn't anywhere near as diligent as many countries on this in any case,"

"So how will the Logan Spencer part work?"

"I'm not completely certain yet. I think we'll somehow need to link the new company with Spencer. That way, when the money disappears, he can take the hit."

"What has Bigsy got to do?" asked Clare.

"We will need a web-site that looks like the corporate site for a Space Exploration Company."

"He will love that," said Clare smiling, "A proper boys' toys project."

"And I guess Jake can write the copy for it," said Christina.

"Let me call them," said Clare, "It'll be so much fun explaining it!"

"I know you will, but please emphasise the secrecy of the whole endeavour," said Christina.

Layover

The seven-hour layover passed fast, courtesy of the hotel facilities. They were soon all back in a different plane, enjoying the experience of First Class travel.

Jallie T's band had all visited the First-Class Lounge in Frankfurt airport, where they had enjoyed free drinks and a further meal.

Jallie T and Ellie had decided to take a wellness visit to the spa and Nate, Raff and Lucas had visited the Cigar Lounge, where they had spotted another well-known band engaged in wholly legal smoking.

"They were obviously quite used to the lifestyle," said Nate, "It made us look less cool. It was obvious that we were lounge virgins."

"And it is strange to be so star-struck, when we saw the other band!"

"You'll get used to it on this tour, I'm sure," answered Christina. She could also notice Lucas, still with a slightly pained expression. Lucas was the one counting the sheep in and out. Trying to remember where all of the moving parts were located.

Eckhart and Irina arrived just as the last call to the gate was being made.

"You two sit together, I'll sit with Clare," suggested Christina. It would make for an easier flight without the need to concentrate on all of the Russian mobster names.

"Great plan," said Irina, as she and Eckhart picked two seats together.

Christina nudged Clare over to the other gangway and they sat together, with Clare having a window seat.

"Are you sure?" asked Clare, "Is' mir egal," answered Christina, "I really don't mind."

"I forgot you spoke German as well," said Clare.

"My time in Berlin," answered Christina, "I speak a curious Brandenburger form of German."

The plane readied for take-off.

"Next stop Tokyo!" exclaimed Eckhart.

# Big in Japan

Tokyo

Finally, they arrived at Tokyo Haneda airport.

"It's like a theme park," said Jallie T.

"Look there's the old town Edo Market," said Nate, and they all looked towards the first level, where restaurants and shops competed for the mostly outgoing passengers' time.

"And we'll need to look at the second level, Tokyo Pop Town - especially being pop stars and all," said Raff, as they wandered towards the exits.

Christina was pleased to see that everyone looked in good spirits after such a long flight, but realised that they would also soon be in their hotel rooms, this time without sharing.

"And we'll be able to meet Erasmus!" said Eckhart,

"It's Erebus," corrected Jallie T, waggling her finger, as everyone laughed.

They headed outside and found the taxi rank. Clare went to the front and asked the taxi-marshal if they could get a couple of big buses to take them with their luggage to the hotel.

Eckhart looked on as Clare swung into road manager mode and then, with Lucas, they soon had their gear and luggage plus the whole band in a couple of large vans.

"Yes, he spoke great English and even welcomed us to Tokyo," said Clare as she returned.

"Before we leave, can someone who knows how much gear we have please just check we've got everything?"

Lucas nodded and jumped out again, checking in both of the vans.

"Yes, it's all here," he said, " I was kinda fretting."

"The drums, amps and other rental equipment should all have been delivered to the venue," said Eckhart.

"It's also a direct route along the motorway to the Hotel. We should get an unobstructed view of the waterfront, as well as of Shinagawa and Minato City. Our hotel, the Andaz, is quite close to the Tokyo Tower.

They left Haneda Airport and were soon speeding along an elevated section of road. "This all looks as if it has only just been built," said Nate.

"I don't know," answered Clare," I know they are still building lots in the area around Minato City. That's where we turn left and if we'd kept going straight ahead we'd be in Ginza."

"Ginza?" said Nate, "That's where all the high end shops are, I think."

"Yes," said Christina, "But quite a few of them are well-known in Europe, so it is a slightly weird experience, in Japan looking at high-end European shops."

"Money attracts money," said Raff. The others laughed.

"So where are we playing the concert?" asked Christina, realising she had it mentally as "'Tokyo' rather than as the exact venue."

"Oh, its somewhere called the Tokyo Dome," said Eckhart, "It's to the north."

"Tokyo dome?" asked Christina, "that's more like a stadium?- are you sure about that?"

Clare looked it up on her iPhone, "Yes, and you'll be following such acts as -er- Michael Jackson, Madonna and Celine Dion!"

"Okay, we may have to play the Canadian card then!" said Raff.

"I'd no idea that Erebus were so big!" said Alex, "We'll have to go large!"

'I hope those rental amps have an 'eleven' setting on them!" said Nate.

Erebus

Inside the hotel was everything they could have hoped for. High-end, stylish and peaceful. Well-mannered gracious staff and a distinct feeling of being pampered. Christina's corner room looked out across the city and towards the water. There was enough room for a round table conference in the room. She wondered how much the FSB had budgeted for this.

They had agreed to meet with the other band in the cocktail bar. Christina took her time and then walked along to the bar. It was quiet, except for one rowdier table in a corner. She looked across and realised it was the band. Jallie T was already there, as were Irina and Eckhart.

"Look, here's Christina!" called out Eckhart, as she approached the table. The band members looked up. She knew they were making an instant assessment of her linked to her being the support act.

"Hey Christina," said one - with a notably Canadian burr to his voice - both friendly and slightly unusual at the same time, "Lets introduce ourselves, I'm Marco, I sing and play guitar, That's Andy - he's a bass player,"

"And some vocals," added Andy.

"Tegan is our other skilled plucker, playing all manner of stringed things."

"Hi," said Tegan, "I was listening to you on the plane on the way over here...sounds great!"

"Then there's Nick. He sits at the back and makes a loud noise!"

"Some call it drumming," said Nick smiling.

"And then our keys, brought to you by the very talented Leroy,"

"I play keys and - I'm sure you'll want to know - synths as well, but not in your electro style."

"Hi and I'm Darius Wakefield, originally from England and the band's manager!"

"You've done well to get such a good tour," said Christina," I was also listening to your music on the flight, I really like that album with a ship on the cover - what was it called - 'Wavelashed? You've got some great riffs going and a good turn of phrase too!"

"It sounds as if we've been studying each other's music!" said Marco, "And I'm embarrassed to say that we are big in Japan! That's how we've got such large venue. Darius even had to negotiate the parking lot split! For us that is a first!"

"Are the gigs in the US a similar scale?" asked Christina. "Only we'd have hired some dancers if we'd known!"

Play On, Christina Nott

Christina noticed that the entire band were dressed in earth tones. Browns, greys and an occasional splash of dark green.

Darius explained, "Actually, the American gigs are smaller. There's a few breakthrough acts that get big in the US. Alanis, Celine, Neil Young, The Wainwrights, Bryan Adams. But most of them have to almost pretend to be Americans to get on well."

Marco continued, "We managed to break through with our album called Border Songs. We probably confused everyone by putting a stars and stripes and a maple leaf flag on it - which was supposed to illustrate the border, but I guess people just saw the American flag."

"That's the one with he big stack of waffles dripping with Maple syrup?" asked Christina.

"Yes - I see you know your album covers!"

"Yes that had 'Seattle' on it and 'Molly in the desert,' which seemed to me to be a strange mix."

"Breaking Bad?" said Marco.

"I got the reference," said Christina. "Molly - aka - MDMA in the desert," and then later that was that line about uncertainty, which was riffing on Heisenberg."

"Very good; We can tell you write your own lyrics, too!" said Marco.

Alex laughed, "And mighty fine lyrics they are too. Those lyrics carried our whole band out here as well!"

Christina was trying to remember which band member Alex was with. Christina decided it must be Marco.

She could see that Eckhart had run out of things to say about pop music as the conversation moved towards specifics and also that Irina looked tuned out from the conversation.

Then Clare arrived with Lucas and they went all around doing introductions again. It had proved a useful icebreaker to have the cocktails. Christina was a little concerned that Irina didn't look her normal buoyant self.

Later in the evening she slid over to ask her, "Hey, is everything okay?"

"I've had a message from Shrike. They will be pulling the meeting forward with the Yakuza to the day after the concert. That's really no problem because we can run it in your hotel suite."

"I wondered why I'd been give such a huge room!" said Christina.

"The worrying things is that the FSB think there is someone tracking you at the moment. Apparently it was related to something in London, but when the advertisements for the concert appeared, it was easy to spot you and the date you will be in Tokyo."

"Okay," said Christina, "I might want to put out some enquiries of my own about this. See if we can put a stop to it. They will hardly miss me on stage at the Tokyo Dome!"

Stadium Rock

They'd taken a bus to the venue. Eckhart had arranged a 24-seater black bus, which looked suitably rock-star with its darkened windows.

"Nice," said Alex, as she hopped aboard. Erebus were waiting for their transport and looked slightly aghast at the transport for Christina and her band.

"Wow! who is your agency again?" asked Nick looking at the transport.

Lucas was busy counting equipment into the back of the vehicle.

"You'll have to tell me whether you are making any money from this tour, it all seems too 'comfortable!'" said Marco, "I know we only gave you the regular fees."

"We've a bit of a backer," answered Christina, "They don't seem to be too short of cash. We can either have a really good time travelling well, or make a few more bucks by travelling at the back of the plane!"

"Ain't that the truth," said Nate.

"Don't get too many ideas," said Alex, "I think we've lucked out on this tour with Christina and her secretive backers."

Eckhart smiled. He knew that the funds from the FSB were minuscule compared with the effect that the primary mission could have. America in the pocket of Russia, delivered via a greedy American politician.

Outside, the Tokyo Dome looked huge. They walked inside. It looked even bigger.

"Oh. My. God!" said Lucas, "Have we ordered enough lights?"

Eckhart nodded, " I think so, I asked them about recent acts and they said they'd had a girl band called BlackPink here. I asked them if they could do something similar for the lights and the main technical guy said it would be straightforward to re-rig the BlackPink set, but without the side banners."

Clare was looking into her phone, as was Lucas. "Here," said Clare, "It is the BlackPink set."

They both peered at Clares's phone.

"Em, it's K-Pop," said Clare, "Korean Pop girl band, a mainly black set with pink lighting."

"You know what," said Lucas, "We can roll with this. They'll know how to rig it, and even where the stage positions need to be marked. I say we re-purpose their light show; we can soon change the colours away from pink. This could work."

A cool-looking technical guy was walking towards them in the middle of the auditorium.

"Hey, I'm Rishi," he bowed and tossed back his long black spikey hair. "You are the band that wanted to do a BlackPink lights and set? Let me tell you something - it looks terrific here and we've got it all mapped out in Q-lab."

"Can we get some of the lighting yes changed from pink to other colours?" asked Lucas.

"Sure, you can do what you like here, once you've got the master packs of lights installed. The secret with the Dome is to use as much of the house as you can. If we don't have to re-rig too much it'll be a whole lot simpler, and it will probably look the best too. But you are the support I think? We'd better see what the Main Act wants first. I can put your lights onto a separate universe though. It'll look cool."

At that moment Erebus arrived.

"Hey look, I'd better go talk to them about their requirements. See you all later."

"Roll with it, seems to be the best option," said Clare towards Lucas.

He nodded. "Yes, that Rishi seems to know what he is doing. If we can piggyback from the K-Pop lighting it could work really well."

Lucas looked towards Eckhart, "I'll be seeing the gear next," he said, "We should check what you have ordered. Make sure there is nothing missing."

Eckhart looked concerned, "I ticked the boxes for the set of instruments we'd need on-stage. They had basic, mid range and high-end options. I thought it best to go for the quality equipment."

Sure enough, on an electrically manoeuvrable stage was piled a range of amplifier cabinets, boxes of microphones and cables. Lucas was looking excited.

"Marshall valve amps, Marshall stacks, Fender and a couple of Orange. This is good equipment."

"I ordered whatever they recommended for each of the musician positions, guitar, bass, vocals, keyboards, even drums, which seemed to need a lot of microphones. Luckily, they were in a kit too. Then it recommended that I should arrange for fold-back speakers for each musician so they could hear one another. I ticked that box as well."

"There's more than enough gear here," said Lucas. And I see we can prewire most of it onto one of these electric stages."

Rishi was talking to Erebus, but called over, "Look those secondary stages are pre-wired with spiders of balanced cable and safety cut-off power" he said.

He gestured to one end of the stage and Lucas took a look.

"This is all preconfigured he said., "It will take the headaches out of setting up the band for a sound-check."

Christina could see that Rishi was having a tougher time with Erebus. They had brought their own programmable lights and wanted to have them hung in a particular layout.

"I can do this, but it will take my riggers a few hours," said Rishi.

Christina could see that Darius, their manager, was making heavy going of getting Erebus configured.

"Let's do a trial setup," said Lucas, and the band nodded in agreement. Unlike many touring bands, they would do their own setups, with hastily assembled guitar racks, a drum kit and a couple of keyboards. Lucas was laying out some cabling, but Christina noticed that most of the band could use radio systems for the guitars and microphones.

"This is so much simpler than our usual setup," said Lucas.

About half an hour passed and the band was configured in much the same way that they had been for the rehearsals.

Lucas asked Rishi about connecting the stage to the main control room and desks.

"Yes just plug through the spider links," he said, "then you should be good to go." He spoke Japanese into his radio and the main stage lights did a kind of flicker.

"Yes you are now hot," he said," you're on automatic lights and have our sound engineer to try out your sound mix. You'd better play something."

Nate plugged in his guitar and wound up the volume.

He plucked the beginning of 'Remember Me.'

It was eight notes. The whole band rocked back on their heels. The sound was filling a stadium. The lights were ripping on in time with the string plucks.

"No way!" said Alex, gasping.

"This is pretty cool!" said Clare.

Ellie pumped away at a few chords of the keyboard track to Remember Me.

The lights flickered again and the sound played back out of the foldback speakers.

"This is amazing!" said Ellie.

"Not a bad sound, considering you have only just done setup," said Rishi, "Mind you your gear is all high-end. What do you think of the lights? I think we can leave the on automatic and maybe just blend in some follow spots for the band members. It should look good, especially for the support band!"

Christina had moved over to the microphone. Let's do Hey DJ, she said and the others nodded.

Ellie's keys came in and then the bass. Jallie T came in on backing vocals and Christina and Jallie-T harmonised.

"Tokyo Club Mix!" said Clare, and they all laughed.

"Wow, your stuff is really good said Rishi, smiling, "You can imagine, we hear all kinds of music here. Yours taps into the mainstream of what people like here! Hey - I have an idea - Can one of you come with me?"

Play On, Christina Nott

Clare nodded to follow Rishi to a door on the edge of the stage area.

"This is where we keep the retail stock," he said, "You can imagine the amount we get through."

"Take a look at this..." He pointed towards a mountain of cardboard boxes piled high along a back wall.

"They are BlackPink mallets, left over from their gig here. We over-ordered."

Clare opened a box and looked at something that resembled a mallet. A black handle and two pink heart shaped hammer areas.

"Yeah, look," Rishi picked one up and tapped the table. Two pink lights sprang up inside the mallet.

Clare looked suspiciously on.

"No that's all it does although if you wave it around the lights start to flash and then when you move it faster they go solid again," said Rishi.

"Look they are not branded, so we could use them in the shop for tonight's gig, as accompaniment foe the Christina Nott section? It would help us out - to shift more of them, and it would make your part of the show quite an occasion? What do you think? I'll even do you a split on them? 70/30? "

Clare paused to consider.

"Okay, 60/40!" said Rishi, "I really want them gone!"

"Done," said Clare and they shook hands.

"That's great, and you'll be amazed how many people will buy these things!" said Rishi.

They walked back to the stage area. Christina and the band were just finishing "Earth." They seemed to have settled into the big sound that they needed to make in the arena.

Clare could see Darius disagreeing with Marco from Erebus. It was something to do with the staging for the show. She had picked up from Alex earlier that there seemed to be tensions in Erebus and that all was not running smoothly.

"We'll need to sign off on the lights and sound sometime soon," said Lucas. "I'm pretty happy, we are using their Dome they way they like to run it, so that's why we are getting such good results. Any objections?" he looked around and everyone seemed perfectly happy.

You know we were probably running the sound at around 2 out of 10, said Rishi. As it gets louder there is more chance of feedback, especially from a forward position."

"That's fine, said Lucas, "I'll make sure the band all know this and that we behave!"

Rishi smiled. Lucas could tell Rishi was pleased with the support band's way of conducting business.

Darius had brought two more of the band into an argument with the riggers now and they were debating about how the spinners would be mounted. Richi walked over and politely explained that they would have to bring down the gantry and that this would cause a delay to completion of the rigging before they could run a sound check.

They still had four hours to show time, so the decision was made to bring down the rigging and to rewire the lighting for Erebus.

"Don't worry about the support band. They are on a separate DMX universe," explained Richi.

"Another planet, more like," someone muttered as Christina and the others walked towards the back of the Dome.

"Time for some refreshment?" asked Irina. They all nodded their agreement.

"Iv've just found an amazing sushi bar across the street!" said Irina.

They walked out of the venue, with Erebus still rigging their set.

Showtime

Evening. The Tokyo Dome. The house CCTV showed that it was filling, slowly at first but as the time for the start approached, it looked as if there would be a high capacity crowd present.

Christina and the band looked at the monitors. They were due on at 20:15 until 20:45. Then a half -hour changeover and the main band Erebus would be on for a scheduled 90 minutes. The Dome had a curfew time of 22:00. Both bands get-out were scheduled until 23:00.

Alex told the band that Erebus had got into some difficulties with the venue. Darius had asked that everything be wired the same way that they were used to in Canada. This has meant bypassing many of the venues standards facilities and then cabling a new equivalent.

The sound check had been hurried and there were still some sound balance questions arising when they finished. Andy, the bassist could not hear the rest of the band on his 'ears' either.

They had run cables across the stage instead of using radio mikes and radio transmitters for the guitars. It had taken them 30 minutes to locate and resolve a hum coming from one of the guitars.

"Compared with our setup, it looks as if Erebus have had a few challenges," observed Clare.

The PA in the changing room crackled. "5 minutes to stage."

They all stood up and Nate reached for his guitar.

There was a gentle tap on the door.

A woman dressed in all black poked her head around the door. She was also wearing a headset.

"Follow me now, to the stage, please" she said quietly.

The band followed her along a twisted path around the back of the stage.

Occasionally they could see white arrows pointing towards the stage. Then they stepped over an area marked out with white hash symbols and on to their electrically controlled stage.

They realised it was already in position. Christina could see Rishi in the wings. He held both thumbs up. They were ready to go.

Nate struck up the opening cards of Hey DJ.

Christina started to sing. There was reassuring bass thump from Ellie. Then Raff's drums. And finally Alex coming in to harmonise with Christina.

The lights worked in sync with the beat, mainly from Ellie. The sound was terrific. And then, suddenly, they saw the pink lights come on from the audience.

Rishi would be pleased. There were hundreds, maybe thousands of the small pink mallets rising and falling in time with the music.

Christina turned to Alex. Alex smiled back.

At the end of the song, Alex said to Christina "Never in a million years did I expect this!"

Ellie started Tell Me What You Want From Me. The lights round the stadium rippled in time with the baseline. The pink mallets adjusted to the time signature of the next song. The band looked at one another smiling. As the song reached its end, Nate and Ellie cleverly wove the start of the next tune into the end of the previous one, so they could go into Feel Your Body All Over Mine.

Rishi was standing in the wings, looking captivated by the sounds. He beamed a thumbs up to Christina, who added 'Thanks Rishi' into the lyrics. He clutched his heart and mimed a swoon.

Christina looked around for Eckhart and Irina. She could see them talking together in the other wings, less engaged in the music.

"This one's for the FANS," she said and they started up Remember Me.

Christina could hear the sound of whoops and screams from the stadium. Her own foldback system was loud enough to drown out most of it, but she was increasingly aware of the reaction.

She looked over to the countdown clock on stage. 03 minutes left. "We've gotta go now," she said, remembering that it would be bad for a support act to steal time from the main attraction.

"She called out Hey DJ, and Nate immediately took up the riff. She was gambling that the audience wouldn't mind hearing the track twice, especially if none of them had heard any of her music before. Sure enough there were whoops of recognition and the band played right up to the end of the countdown. Finishing on a Nate power chord and the sizzle from one of Raff's cymbals.

"Thank you I've been Christina Nott and this is the Jallie T Band!" called Christina as they all bowed and walked from the stage.

Rishi ran over.

"That was awesome!" He said,"It feels a privilege to be here during your show. Thank you so much." He did a little bow.

Christina said, "Come here!" she grabbed his hand and then hugged him. "Thank you too, for being so helpful to us!" she said as he looked confused and walked away.

She could sense the tension increasing as Erebus came to the stage. Electricians and Riggers ran around. Darius was shouting instructions and a couple of roadies were still tuning the drums and guitars on stage.

The audience had settled into a happy buzz, with occasional flickers of light from the remaining illuminated mallets.

"Whose idea were those pink lights?" asked Alex," They were incredible!"

"It was Rishi who had a shed-full to sell, I'm sure he must be very happy now!" said Clare.

"And Ellie - you had so much power in those bass notes...to colour a whole stadium!"

"I know, it was the coolest thing!" she said. It was clear the whole band were basking in the afterglow of a great gig.

They looked towards the stage and could see the continued frenetic behaviour of Erebus trying to assemble itself for the start. There was shouting between the touring roadies and the Dome crew.

"This isn't going to help anyone," said Christina.

"Stay out of it," advised Clare.

Christina nodded.

The start time arrived but the band were still not ready. They could hear the crowd getting restless, especially after an entertaining first act.

Then, some ten minutes late, the band walked on. They plugged in, but looked a little dejected, like they had already given up before they started.

Play On, Christina Nott

The drummer tapped his sticks together one-two-three and the band eased into their first track. It was a well-known hit single and something of an anthem for the band.

"There's no bass." said Lucas, "The bass player is playing but there's no bass from the main system."

Erebus continued oblivious to the end of the first number. Lucas waved to Rishi. Rishi caught his eye. "No bass," he mouthed. He pointed to the bass player and did a crossed arms gesture.

Richi understood and climbed onto the stage. Lucas could see Rishi fiddling around with various control leads. Then he saw a row of lights come on.

"Huh, they only left the amp unplugged!" he said to Christina.

Finally, Erebus were fully functional, some fifteen minutes after the start time for their set.

Christina could tell that they were accomplished musicians well-used to playing together and to the vagaries of a live set. Unfortunately, it came across as slightly lack-lustre, as if someone was slowing down the speed of each track.

The audience were still appreciative and whooped and cheered at the right points. But to Christina it felt as if they were playing a long set of slightly bored sounding music. Like they knew their tunes but had become disaffected with them.

Finally, they brought in their other hit single as a finale, but Christina wondered whether their music had all been at one level, instead of showing light and shade.

She wondered if they would do an encore, because they still had 8 minutes on the clock and sure enough they left the stage, waited for the foot stomping and came back to play one more track, a more lively rock-n-roller which got everyones' feet stomping.

Then, a final chorus and the last crescendo of notes. They had brought the Erebus music train into the station.

The stadium erupted into noise and cheers and almost simultaneously the house lights came up and background music appeared from the speakers. The concert was well-and-truly over.

Lucas appeared and signalled, "We'll need to start the get out." The entirety of Christina Nott's stage had been electronically moved to the wings on Stage Left and it was a relatively easy matter to disconnect everything and to compare with the house for who owned which pieces of kit. The guys from the equipment hire company had reappeared as well and were studiously reclaiming all of their expensive amplifiers and other equipment.

Rishi reappeared, "You nailed it," he said, "Come down to Club heavysick ZERO after this tonight. I can get you on stage. They will love you. Wait afterwards and I'll take you there."

Alex looked at Christina, "Please and can we do something as Jallie T too?" she asked imploringly.

"Sure, I'm in," said Christina looking over at Clare - who nodded and Irina who did a 'don't know' raised hands gesture.

Marco, from Erebus appeared, "Hey you did a good set tonight! What were all of those hammers about? Something to do with K-Pop, I'm told. And its great that it is giving Alex a chance to strut her stuff too!" He lightly kissed Alex on the cheek.

"We're off to a Japanese Club!" she announced, "heavysick ZERO - we've been offered a gig there."

"Wow - what tonight?" asked Marco, "I thought you'd be back at the hotel?"

"I will later. But this opportunity is too good to miss," said Alex.

Lucas reappeared, "We're all done. I just need to load it back onto the bus now. Eckhart, can you help me for a moment?"

Eckhart nodded and Christina could hear Lucas flattering Eckhart for his choice of equipment.

Heavysick ZERO

"Are we taking the bus?" asked Lucas - to the Club?

"Yes there's plenty of parking across the street," said Rishi.

Rishi spoke to their driver. He laughed when he heard Rishi say the name of the club. He nodded. It was obvious he knew where it was located.

"Nakano," he said, "Past Shinjuku!"

They drove for a while and everyone was aware of the increasingly searing bright lights as they approached Shinjuku. They could see the pavements crushed under the sheer volume of pedestrians.

Alex looked around, she'd brought Marco along, but the other members of Erebus had decided to go their own way to a late bar in Shinjuku.

"It's the busiest train station in the world here at Shinjuku," said Rishi, "Look there's the entrance to Kabukicho," He pointed to a big red neon sign over a street lit with many more neon signs.

"Is that what I think it is?" asked Christina, gesturing towards the street.

"Red Light? Yes. Plus Karaoke bars and other things."

"It looks extremely tacky, " observed Clare.

"Full of tourists and young, shy, Japanese business men- the salarymen," explained Rishi., "The long hours working and karōshi-avoiding male workers. It is still a very gendered culture here in Japan."

" Karōshi?" asked Clare.

"Yes, it is death by overwork," explained Rishi, "And surprisingly common. They had to bring in a new Law, which sets limits on overtime to 45 hours a month. That's high anyway, and 'highly skilled professionals' are exempt from this protection, and that's what most salarymen aspire to be."

The bus was slowing into a parking lot.

"The club is just across the way from here," explained Rishi, "I rang ahead to say that I'd got the 'great Christina Nott and her band,' and that you would do a short guest spot here tonight."

As they climbed out of the bus, Christina could see that Clare had put an arm around Lucas.

"Austin rules tonight?" she suggested to Clare. Clare looked back, "Yep. Austin rules. What happens in heavysick ZERO stays in heavysick ZERO!"

Christina felt Rishi touching her hand as they walked towards the club.

Austin Rules

"I expect there's a different word for death from overindulgence?" said Clare as she knocked at the door of Christina's room. It was late morning.

Christina answered, "Hiya - I think we missed the land of the rising sun," she smiled as Clare entered. Rishi was sitting at a table eating a small meal. It looked like rice, grilled fish, miso soup, pickles and a delicately sliced omelette.

"Breakfast," he explained, "They serve a great Japanese breakfast here. I'll be going after I've finished this. That was some show last night, I loved that Alex and also you, Clare, were up on stage! You should teach me those moves!"

Clare looked across to Christina.

"Austin rules," said Christina.

"Yes it did get kind of crazy towards the end," said Clare.

"How's Lucas?" asked Christina.

"He's back in his room. I think he blew a fuse or something," said Clare, smiling.

"And my boss will blow a fuse if I don't get across to the Dome right now!" said Rishi, looking at his phone, "We've another band coming in from England - I hope they have better manners than that Darius from Erebus!"

Rishi picked up his jacket and started to leave the room. Then, remembering, he turned to Christina and gave her a big kiss.

"Thank you for that special evening!" he said as they parted company. Christina smiled, "See you the next time I'm in Japan!"

"I'll be watching your band from now on!" said Rishi, "Don't be surprised to see me show up at a gig somewhere!"

He walked towards the door, Christina followed him outside for a few moments. Clare looked at the time on her phone as Christina re-appeared.

"I thought I'd better make sure you were up-and-about before Irina and Eckhart arrive at midday. We've got to talk over the setup for the meeting this evening."

"Yes, I think it is Eckhart who has been the fixer for the meeting."

Yakuza

Twelve o' clock and there was a punctual knock on Christina's door. Christina answered and Eckhart and Irina entered.

"This is spectacular!" said Eckhart as he looked at the double aspect windows looking over Tokyo. And there's a meeting space and a separate room for the bed. Excellent as a meeting room suite.

"You'll be meeting with the Inagawa-kai (稲川会) That's the third largest Yakuza family in Japan, with roughly 15,000 members divided into 313 clans. It is based in the Tokyo-Yokohama area and was one of the first Yakuza families to expand its operations outside of Japan. That's how we have a direct contact with them. Through their links in Saint Petersburg. The Inagawa-kai has its headquarters is in Minato City, exactly where they want to build the new tower.

"We are meeting Saito Eiji, who is the leader of the Minato City development. We invited him to your gig yesterday Christina, to a VIP area, where he could see. We explained that he would meet you, today, here in the hotel.

"We have to assume that Saito Eiji is running corruption. More specifically, the use of public office for private gains. Something akin to what Putin appeared to be doing in Saint Petersburg, except Eiji has Yakuza support and the way that the Japanese do it is sometimes more blatant. For example, in this new building, he will want several floors to be handed over for use by government departments. That will ingratiate him to the state and no doubt give him further leverage in the future."

"This all sounds very plausible," said Clare.

"Exactly," answered Irina, " We want Spencer's men to believe that there is a real deal here to be done."

"What will the roles be?" asked Christina, "Am I playing security?"

"That's right," said Eckhart, "You and me both. Saito Eiji will bring his own security, but he suggested that we have some as well. He said it will make him look stronger to have overseas security in the room."

"What about Spencer?" asked Christina.

"He'll bring a lawyer, and maybe one or two backup body guards. They won't expect the kind of hardcore security that Saito Eiji brings. After all, Eiji is playing on his home field here."

"And Clare?"

"Clare, my darling, you should go back to your room. No sense in rattling either party by us having too many people in the room."

Clare nodded. She knew when Christina was working it was sometimes better to be out of the way.

"One thing though," said Clare, "I saw pictures of Logan Spencer today from some sort of campaigning he'd been doing. He's managed to insult the local native Americans, who happened to be hosting a speaking event in one of their casino and conference facilities. It is all over Twitter."

Irina nodded towards Eckhart, "It looks as if you were right, Spencer will be sending someone else to negotiate for him. He's showing the Yakuza that he's too busy and self-important to be showing up in Tokyo for a meeting."

"Aside from that being fairly insulting, I guess the session can still go ahead. We need to put the bait on the hook!" said Eckhart.

"Okay, so should we get the room prepared? Quiet opulence is the order of the day. We'd better order some Champagne and hard liquor."

"And fill me in on the Yakuza," asked Christina, "All I know is that they have their little fingers chopped off!"

Eckhart started to explain, "I had to look them up too. Hundreds of years ago, they started out as outcasts - wandering peddlers who traveled from village to village, selling low-quality goods at festivals and markets.

By the 1700s, they began to organise into tight-knit groups under the leadership of bosses and underbosses. That's when they started early organised crime, such as protection rackets.

Later, the shogun's government sought to calm the gang wars between them and they appointed new bosses to oversee what they were doing.

The second group that makes the Yakuza was formed from gamblers. Gambling was strictly forbidden during Tokugawa times and remains illegal in Japan to this day.

They took to the highways, fleecing unsuspecting marks with dice or card games. They often had colourful tattoos all over their bodies, which led to the custom of full-body tattooing for modern-day yakuza. From their core business as gamblers, they branched out into loan sharking and other illegal activities.

After World War II, the Yakuza gangs rebounded in strength. The Japanese government estimated in 2007 that there were more than 102,000 Yakuza members working in Japan and abroad, in 2,500 different families.

Many Yakuza sport full-body tattoos which are made with traditional bamboo or steel needles, rather than modern tattooing guns.

"And Christina is right about the loss of finger joints. It is traditionally supposed to make the gangster's sword grip weaker, theoretically leading him to depend more on the rest of the group for protection. Today, many yakuza members wear prosthetic fingertips to avoid being conspicuous."

"I knew it!" said Christina.

Eckhart continued, "The Inagawa-kai - who we are meeting - operate out of Tokyo and Yokohama, with 15,000 members. They engage in criminal activities such as international drug-smuggling, human trafficking, and arms smuggling. Remember they hold the keys to Minato City.

"They have made themselves look legitimate too, haven't they?" asked Clare.

Eckhart nodded, "Yes, they also hold significant amounts of stock in large, legitimate corporations, and some have close ties with the Japanese business world, the banking sector, and the real estate market."

Irina added, "Frankly, that Logan Spencer would even be holding a meeting with the Yakuza is a scandal waiting to be discovered."

Saito Eiji

There was a knock on the door. Christina answered it. A dark suited Japanese man entered without saying anything. Then another followed him into the room. Christina was not phased by the theatrics. It was like a basic security class back at the Academy.

"We are security ahead of Saito Eiji san and Furukawa Haruhiro san," he stated.

Christina noticed that both of the security seemed quite short. She assumed they were also fast.

"Do you carry weapons?" she asked.

"Yes," said the same man. He didn't offer to say what they were carrying.

Christina assessed they would both have pistols and some form of martial weapon, probably knives.

There was further noise at the door and then several men entered.

Three of the men wore the same dark suits as the two men already in the room. One man carried a large submachine gun on a strap across his back. The third suited man was significantly older than the other men. Christina assumed he was the lawyer.

And the last man in the room was wearing a wide-checked overcoat, a light brown leather hat and Ray-Ban Aviator type sunglasses. This had to be Saito Eiji san.

"Good afternoon," he said, "And you must be Christina Nott. I am pleased to meet you. Mr Bloch arranged for us to have VIP seats at the Tokyo Bowl yesterday. He said we would visit you here at your suite for the meeting with Logan Spencer. You must come along to one of my venues or my parties soon, we very much enjoyed your part of the show."

Eckhart stepped forward, "Yes, I'm afraid we could not arrange for you to meet the rest of the band. Here is my colleague Irina Morozova, she is running the security here, to support your own excellent men."

"I cannot see security here?" said Sato Eiji.

"Then we are doing our job," said Irina bowing to Eiji, "It looks better that you have your own men visible."

"From the Sankt Petersburg Bratva, I thank you for your assistance with this. You know that Logan Spencer has sent his spokesperson along?"

"Yes, we saw he was somewhere in Minnesota making further stupid statements on Twitter. I'm not sure really why anyone does business with him. I don't think he could run corner shop," said Eiji.

"Let me introduce you also to my lawyer, Furukawa Haruhiro san," he gestured towards him and there was more bowing around the room.

"I am sorry, but we mean no disrespect that we have no business cards to offer to you, but our normal business doesn't seem use them," said Irina.

"That is fine, I will settle for a signed copy of Christina Nott's CD instead, and maybe one for Haruhiro san, please."

Christina nodded, now she would need to text Clare to find a couple of copies.

"There was another knock on the door.

"Please take seats around the large table," said Irina to Eiji san.

Christina answered the door again and a large man with a curly wired earpiece came in.

"Christina Nott? We are here with Kayden Lowe, who is representing Logan Spencer. Please show me everyone who will be here for the meeting."
  "No, no, no," thought Christina, "This is no way to run civilised security. Too brash."

"Okay, but first can you tell me if you are carrying a weapon?" asked Christina.

"Glock 19" came the reply, but no attempt to show it.

CIA weapon of choice, thought Christina.

"Nice piece of Austrian engineering!" she said, as she watched the American look confused.

There was further noise at the door and the rest of the group walked in. In the middle was Kayden Lowe, young-looking, sporting an expensive Bvlgari gold watch. Christina guessed it would cost over $20,000.

She remembered that Kayden Lowe was some kind of relative of Logan Spencer. Then she remembered that Spencer liked to keep the business in the family.

"Myron Reinharz is our lawyer here, who am I talking to?" Asked Kayden Lowe.

Christina was taken aback with the arrogance and lack of manners of Lowe.

Less taken aback or so it seemed, was Saito Eiji. He went through the bowing ritual and presented a business card to Lowe, who took the pacing and slowed down a little in his own delivery.

Christina had seen it so many times before, as two alpha males squared off for a business negotiation.

"Well, we think we have an interesting proposition for Mr Spencer," said Saito, "We would like to be able to brand our new block as one of his towers. Spencer Towers Tokyo. We believe this will help us sell the towers to the Russians and Americans. Our proposition is laid out in this prospectus and we will need an answer within one week from today.

"Just what are you offering?"

Branding, in return for an 18% stake in the building, but payable as a direct fee. Options to purchase up to 1/3 of the apartments for resale at 60% of the retail price. Options to provide construction and maintenance services on the new Tower.

And what is the estimated construction cost of the building?" asked Lowe.

"We think it will cost around $1 billion to construct, so your 18% would be around $180 million.

"We think the mark-up on the apartments will be 100%, so with 10 prime estate apartments retailing at $50 million and another 40 at $10 million, that is $900 million of apartments available at 1/3 share and 60% of retail. It works out to $99.9 million for the share in the large apartments and $79.92 million for the share in the smaller apartments.

"You get given the cash for the brand up-front which is enough to buy all of your apartment shares when the Tower is finished.

"I think you Americans have an expression for it. "Money for old rope,"

"What is the catch?"

Saito replied, "There is no catch. We want to put up 1/3 of the investment in the new tower. We could afford to put it all up, but it would draw too much attention to us in our home city. Instead, we want Spencer to persuade the other two investors to go ahead. That would be maybe one or two meetings. It is a good hourly rate."

And when would we receive the initial payment?"

"I suggest you read the prospectus. But the initial payment is as soon as the two other investors have paid their down payment Phase 1 percentages to get the project started."

"And Mr Lowe. We are not desperate for Spencer to do this. We offer it as a polite consideration for him. If there is any dithering or delay, we will move our options elsewhere. We have several other people interested. No. Very interested in this transaction."

Lowe looked towards his lawyer Reinharz questioningly.

"This all seems to be in order, " said Reinharz.

"Okay, we will leave now, I must discuss this with other interested parties with Spencer Industries."

Lowe stood, as did Reinharz and his security. They walked towards the door.

Irina opened it for them to go outside into the corridor.

"Welle, it doesn't look as if they liked the refreshments on offer," said Saito Eiji san.

Christina, smiled, she kind of liked Eiji, even if he was a ruthless mobster.

"Well, Eiji-san asked, "Was that a good enough 'show' for you? Personally, I found Kayden Lowe to be a 少したわごとをジャンプ.

"I assume it is best that we don't know the translation for that?" smiled Christina.

"Christina Nott. You are funny. Very amusing. Yes. And you are quite right."

There was a gentle tap on the door. Christina realised it was Clare with several CDs.

She answered the door, said "Don't come in, just hand them to me...Love you. Thanks."

Christina returned to the table, where EIji-san and his gang were now standing.

"Here's the CD. What shall I sign?" asked Christina.

Eiji-san smiled, "just 'love Christina' would be fine!"

"Okay - but let me insist that we take a selfie as well," she said and closed in on him for a picture, "There I've taken one, now we can ask your security to take another."

Eiji-san gestured to the original English-speaking short suited security man and he took the picture.

Christina noticed a smile of delight as he took it and realised that these security guards were still young.

"Here," she said and gestured to him, "For you." She kissed the CD box and left traces of her lipstick. The guard looked to Eiji-san.

"You have another CD?" he asked, "Then give that one to me and the next to him."

Christina kissed another box, hoping her lipstick would hold out.

Play On, Christina Nott

Hardboiled

"Chance is life's only certainty."

— Mickey Wyte

Debrief

"Well, that seemed to go okay?" suggested Christina.

"I agree, although Kayden Lowe is somewhat hardboiled," said Irina.

"I should think that Kayden lives in a shadow world of fear, created by Logan Spencer. He's probably not allowed to have his own mind, and I expect that Spencer would steal his shadow if he thought that possible," observed Christina.

"Wow, you don't have a lot of time for Spencer," said Irina.

Christina nodded, "He's created his own version of the truth, which he fervently believes. Somehow, he is managing to spread the same unattractive future towards many of the people who he is, in reality, stealing from. I'm not sure who is the bigger corrupter, Putin or Spencer?"

"I'm glad we are having this conversation in Tokyo, and not in Saint Petersburg," said Irina, "It could get very difficult there - where the walls have ears."

Eckhart added, "Yes, I think we now have Kayden hooked. Who wouldn't go for that deal? Give them money, and then offer them discounted hotel rooms which they can buy back for the same amount? - I wish I could get a deal like that!"

"No, it is only the immensely corrupt that get offered such deals," murmured Clare, "And it doesn't even look like something too good to be true to them, either."

"It was fairly typical that Spencer sent along one of his men to hold the discussions though," said Eckhart.

"I think he actually sent one of his rudest employees; I could not believe how discourteous they were to Saito Eiji-san," said Christina.

"Well, admittedly he is also a piece of work," said Clare, " We'll have to remember whose side we are on during all of this!

"Always, " said Christina, and noticed that both Eckhart and Irina nodded.

Tokyo Andez Hotel

Downstairs in the main bar of the of the Tokyo Andaz Hotel. Christina and Clare were sitting chatting when Jallie T walked in.

"Hi Christina, Clare," she said, "I've news. It's a bit awkward really."

"What is it, Alex? " asked Christina, looking worried.

"Well, you might have noticed that the Erebus part of the gig at the Dome was somewhat choppy?"

"Well, there were a few hiccups setting everything up, " acknowledged Clare

"Yes, Darius and Marco have had a big bust-up. Marco wanted to go with the standard set-top at the Dome, but Darius insisted on using all of their own equipment. We think he's got some kind of financial interest in doing that."

"Well, it all seemed to get resolved before they went on stage though, didn't it?" said Clare.

"They were ten minutes late starting and if you remember the bass didn't work. It had been left unplugged."

"Oh, yes, I remember, Lucas told Rishi there was no bass and he went on stage to fix it," answered Clare.

"Well their 'ears' were not working properly either. They couldn't hear what one another were playing."

"I thought it was because of where we were standing," said Christina, "It seemed slightly out of synchronisation."

"No, it was properly out of sync. They have a house recording and listened to it back yesterday and it was obvious that they'd got it wrong," said Alex. "Marco was furious with Darius, but then Darius said it was because everyone at the venue had been distracted by the Christina Nott Band, as he called it."

"Does he know that - you two?" asked Christina, " Oh yes, but anyway Darius has thrown all of toys out of the pram. He wants to go on the next leg of the tour without you. He wants to pick up a local band instead for Australia."

"What about beyond?" asked Clare.

"Well, that's where it gets difficult," replied Alex, "He can't throw you out of the American leg. For a couple of reasons. First of all, it is a different promotor for the American circuit but just as importantly, we crushed it at the Tokyo Dome and its reached mainstream media. The pictures from the gig and the YouTube clips are everywhere - the scenes with those mallets! Thank goodness they were unbranded or we'd have BlackPink down on us."

Clare decided for tactical reasons to keep quiet about the little arrangement she'd made with Rishi about the surplus stock.

"So do we need to get some of that merchandise over to the USA?" asked Eckhart, "I didn't order it for the tour."

"I think Rishi might be able to help," suggested Clare, "I think he knows how to get his hands on a supply."

"That's great! I'll call him later, We just need to get them shipped over to LA."

"So our next stop is going to be L.A?" Asked Christina.

"We'll be rested and relaxed by the time Erebus arrive," said Clare.

"Er, that's what I was going to mention," said Alex, "I'm thinking of going along with Erebus to Sydney and then joining you again in L.A."

Irina looked at Eckhart, "What about the rest of the band?" she asked

"Oh, no, they will be ready to come along straight to Los Angeles, I'm tagging along with Marco."

"That's all fine, although we'd arranged for you to share rooms again in Los Angeles," said Eckhart, "On account of it being at the Roosevelt, which is a proper celebrity spot just off Hollywood Boulevard."

"I'd love to be along, but I should stay with Marco and try to patch things up between our bands. I suggest you don't tell Darius about you staying at the Roosevelt though, he's jealous enough of your touring style!"

Spanner

London. Evening. A phone call.

"Yes, she was there. Playing on stage with her own band. They are part of the Erebus Tour. Next stop is Sydney, Australia."

"Good, you'll have local people there to take care of things. The next show is at the Qudos Bank Arena. No, Q.U.D.O.S. It is very well known. It is advertised on the internet, but only says 'with support'."

"Okay."

The line clicked. It was the end of the call.

*

Identified

Tokyo Andaz Hotel. Christina was looking out across the lights of Tokyo.

Her phone blipped. It was a text. An 001 number. One word.

"Chuck".

She picked up the phone and pressed dial.

A click from the other end.

"Chuck?" she asked,

"Hey Christina, that was fast! Too much time on your hands?" asked Chuck.

Chuck Manners and Christina had history. Him a freelance agent for the CIA and she operating for the FSB, yet somehow brought together through mutual acquaintances.

"No, I'm in the middle of a music tour actually," answered Christina, "Are you okay?"

"I know about your tour," answered Chuck. "It is because of it that I'm calling you. Remember that time with puffin and penguin?"

"Auk and Puffin," corrected Christina, "When there were two agents tailing you, I seem to remember an incident in a hotel room in Brussels when they finally caught up with you!"

"Yes, that's right and you came in all guns blazing! I even bought the same model submachinegun afterwards-in black though."

"Well, it turns out that it has triggered some heavy duty surveillance. They tailed you into London, sloppily didn't get anything useful and then wanted to follow you to bring you in."

"Who are 'They'?" asked Christina.

"Oh sorry, I forgot to say - NATO. They have been following the links back. It goes all the way back to the Minerva Listening Station that the FSB set up in London. You'll remember that lazily the contractors sent to find me - Auk and Puffin - were commissioned from Minerva."

"I remember, it shows how flimsy the intel is, when they are making the kind of links that they have!" observed Christina.

"Yes, well they think you know about some of the secrets that Minerva discovered, particularly on UK Members of Parliament and European Diplomats."

"It's ridiculous!" said Christina, "Minerva was a huge operation with many staff. That I would know anything from it is huge stretch of someone's imagination."

"I guess it could be linked with Bernard Driscoll?" said Chuck, "Remember he was under their watchful eye."

"So what are they expecting to do? Bundle me into the back of a van and take me to an interrogation point?"

"I imagine so - anyway - it is why I contacted you. To warn you that something was being engineered. Word has it that they lost you in London. Then they found you again - cleverly they spotted the thirty-foot-high signs outside the Tokyo Dome, and someone has alerted them to your whereabouts. I think they will try something in Sydney. I was going to offer to come over as another ring of security. The least I could do!"

"Chuck, that is very kind, but between you and me, I'm not going to be in Sydney - the other band cancelled our appearance - I think we stole the show and their manager is jealous."

"We are planning to come over to the USA next, I'll be in LA, at the Roosevelt."

"Ah I see you are learning about the best locations!" smiled Chuck.

"So where are you at the moment?" asked Christina, expecting Chuck to be somewhere in Europe.

"I'm in Albuquerque," answered Chuck, almost sheepishly.

"What? You're back on your old stamping grounds?" asked Christina.

"Yes, they gave me some kind of a mission which leads me across the border. I get to play with a few new toys too - The Phoenix - it's the Alliance Ground Surveillance Force RQ-4D remotely piloted aircraft."

"Alliance Ground Surveillance Force? That's NATO isn't it?"

"Very good, you don't miss anything. Yes it's because of NATO that I got to hear about the word being out on you. Someone in Brussels is bent out of shape because of what they think Minerva discovered."

"So that's the real reason... Covering tracks... as usual!" said Christina, "But I wonder who it could be?"

"I didn't get that information," said Chuck.

"Well, with these flying blobs you'll be doing regular spies out of a job soon enough, " said Christina, "I'm not sure I know about the RQ-4D - is it another flying nose?"

"Yes, think of the Global Hawk on steroids," said Chuck, "But without the V shaped tail."

"So it is really ugly then?" said Christina.

"Confidential," said Chuck, "Look, I'm so close to L.A., I might as well come over. It would be good to see Christina Nott in concert."

"You'll always be welcome and I'll ask for an AAA pass for you."

"Access All Areas! In plain sight - now there's a thing!" said Chuck, "See ya,"

A click and he was gone.

Galactix

Morning and everything was bustling. Erebus were about to leave for Sydney and Alex was going with them. The rest of her band were excitedly talking about Hollywood and some of the sights of Los Angeles.

Irina and Eckhart were talking quietly in one corner of the lobby. Christina had told Clare about the phone call from Chuck. Clare had also news from Bigsy.

"He's built the website for the Space Company, he says he modelled it on SpaceX and Blue Origin."

"Blue Origin?" asked Christina.

"Yes the Jeff Bezos Amazon company for space exploration."

"Oh - how silly of me. Amazon Prime on Mars!"

"Longer delivery times," said Clare, "Well I had a look at Bigsy's website. I was expecting it to look like something from Thunderbirds, but it is actually pretty good. Bigsy has used some really cool NASA shots and a few models. I cross-checked with SpaceX and realised that they use models and CGI too. I'd actually say that Bigsy's is better."

"What's the company called?" asked Christina.

Clare looked at Christina, "After SpaceX and Blue Origin...Presenting...Galactix!"

"Galactix...has a kind of ring to it! Not bad Bigsy!" said Christina.

"He has also ripped off a few press releases from the space exploration companies and judiciously inserted Logan Spencer. It is all looking entirely plausible."

At that moment Irina and Eckhart came over.

"Something we think you should know," said Irina, "We think there is someone following you. We don't know who or where they are from, but our FSB links tell us that they are following your trail."

Christina pretended to be surprised, "Okay - what can we do about it?" she asked.

"I guess Eckhart and I will need to run some extra security for the next leg of the tour," said Irina.

Christina could see Eckhart monitoring the hotel lobby.

Dreamliner

They were on the Dreamliner. The whole band was in Business Class for this leg of the journey, flying on American Airlines.

"This reminds me of British Airways Business Class," said Clare to Christina.

"Yes, it's better than the old-style Business Class on AA," agreed Christina.

The Dreamliner quietly took off and they were soon cruising at 32,000 feet.

"Around ten and a quarter hours flight time," said Christina.

"I might watch a movie," answered Clare, "Or two."

Los Angeles

"Los Angeles was the kind of place where everybody was from somewhere else and nobody really dropped anchor...

People drawn by the dream, people running from the nightmare...

Everybody in L.A. keeps a bag packed. Just in case."

Michael Connelly

LAX

Now, they had landed in L.A. They had a by-now-familiar black bus pick them up from the airport and whisk them to the hotel.

Inside, the Roosevelt was a dark, cool oasis at one end of Hollywood Boulevard. In a few moments, the band had discovered the idyllic pool at the back, designed by David Hockney and surrounded by palm trees.

"This is a magical place," said Clare to Christina, "And we are right in the middle of where the action is!"

"Yes," said Eckhart, "Although its about a half-hour ride to the venue from here."

"We don't have to be there for four days though," said Irina, "We should try to get the meeting with Spencer brought forward."

Eckhart nodded, "I've already been onto that. I've spoken to Bakir Jamalov, Oliver Trask and even Pavle Darchidze can make Thursday. Now we just need Spencer or one of his underlings to agree."

"Where would we hold the meeting?" asked Christina.

"I fixed us a venue. It's Spago and they have a private area where we can eat discreetly," said Eckhart, "It is also useful from a security perspective, because we can control the access."

"Spago?" said Clare, "That's Wolfgang Puck, isn't it?"

"That's right, nothing but the best for our guests," said Eckhart.

"Do you think this will be enough to lure Spencer?" asked Clare.

"I doubt it, " said Christina, "Popular legend has it that Spencer prefers burgers and fries."

"Well, we just need the confirmation from Spencer and we are all set. Remember, this time the other partners are not so keen to join in, which will leave Spencer hanging."

"I can't wait!" said Christina.

Thursday morning

They were all together eating breakfast in the Roosevelt's main restaurant. There was a call from across the way.

"Christina!" She looked over. It was Chuck.

"I just got into town. I flew into LAX and made my way straight here. Wouldn't want to miss the breakfast! He, it is great to see you!"

They hugged, Chuck looked around,"Clare!" he exclaimed, "This is a surprise! - Last time we were in the USA together we were driving around Santa Fe, I seem to remember!"

Clare grinned, stood and walked towards Chuck. She hugged him and was sure she saw some dust curl up from his check shirt.

"These are my other special friends, Chuck, from Saint Petersburg - its Irina and Eckhart, who have arranged most of the tour!"

"Great to meet you both!" said Chuck, then looking over to the band. "And you must be the great Jallie T Band that I've heard so much about!" he said, holding out a hand.

Ellie stood first and said, "Come on - a hug like Christina's - I'm Ellie ! " and stretched her arms out. A brief hug and Clare noted there was more dust in the air.

"I guess Christina didn't mention me?" said Chuck. "I sometimes work with Christina, as Clare knows, but this time I'm here for the music. And hi guys, but I think you are missing Jallie T? Or am I mistaken?"

"I'm impressed," said Christina, "You worked it out!"

"It's all about the music!" said Chuck.

Clare didn't believe a word of it, knowing Chuck's preference for Morgan Wallen singing about Whiskey Glasses, Carrie Underwood singing about Cheatin' Men, and Luke Somebody-or-other singing about Trucks. Many hours crossing deserts with Chuck - oh, for some Eagles.

"So what are ya'll doing?" asked Chuck.

"Secrets," said Christina, "Deep secrets."

"Gotcha," said Chuck, "I can eat this maple stack over there if you'd prefer!"

"Yeah? What secrets?" asked Ellie, in all innocence. Clare realised that they had kept the whole of the Spencer Plan from Jallie T's Band..

"We are pursuing a few business opportunities as well, whilst we are here," explained Christina, "Clare, you and the band will have to make your own entertainment on Thursday evening when we have the main business meeting."

"Sure thing," said Clare, "We'll find somewhere to go!"

"But you'll be joining us?" asked Eckhart, "Oh yes, Christina and I know how one another operate," said Chuck, sinking back into his Texan drawl.

Christina looked at Irina, who seemed to be weighing the options. "Chuck can be just as handy as me in a negotiation," she said, "and mighty trustworthy too."

"In that case, welcome Chuck!" said Irina.

Thursday Evening

"You know something? I'm gonna ride shotgun tonight," announced Chuck, "You have got the private dining covered with all of you. I'm going to be downstairs at a regular table. That way I can see who comes and goes and if there is any additional backup presence. Let me get to the restaurant about an hour ahead of all of you. I can soon tell if anyone else is being moved in to do a similar job to me."

Irina and Eckhart agreed. It would also cut them the greatest freedom.

Two town cars arrived. Chuck took one alone. No sense in arriving with the others and tipping anyone off.

Eckhart, Irina and Christina took the second. By the time the L.A. traffic had sliced and diced, they would be sure of separate arrival times.

They arrived at Spago some 25 minutes later. It was already bustling and the valet parking outside was doing a roaring trade, moving high end pretty cars off to the separate parking lot. The tall, thin and glamorous were arriving in their droves.

Through the doors and they were greeted with an unquestionably high-end aroma of cooking and the occasional waft of expensive perfumes.

"A little piece of Europe," said Christina, as Eckhart and Irina nodded, "I think it is the garlic and herbs that make it seem so familiar! And the wine in the food! Delicious!"

They were shown through to a private dining room, with capacity for around a dozen people to be seated comfortably at a long oval table.

They discussed seating, took seats and waited for their guests to arrive. Once again, their 'friendly' crew had been organised to be 45 minutes ahead of the Spencer group.

Pavle was first to arrive. He greeted them all and asked how everyone had been, "It's very convenient to have the meeting here in L.A.," he said, "I spend maybe half a year here - every year. And I still enjoy Spago too. It's like an old friend, a familiar restaurant where you can go 'off-menu' - something we Californians like. That reminds me - I'll probably have one of Wolfgang's Wiener Schnitzel as we are here. With his lovely Spaetzle, just the way Arnie likes!"

"You know Bakir Jamalov quite well too?" asked Irina, "and are sure he knows the story?"

"Oh yes, and we even talked about it yesterday, by phone. It is surprising how many people have been crossed by Logan Spencer over the years and so an opportunity to get one back on him is to be relished."

"Have you brought any security?" asked Eckhart.

"I put them downstairs," said Pavle, "On the table next to your American friend...Colonel Manners, isn't it?"

Christina stiffened at this.

"Don't worry, you have to consider that this is kind of my town, and so we'd picked up that Manners was on his way here when he booked the flight. I don't know why he didn't travel under an alias or something?

"We could simply pick him up from the airport and watch him all the way here. You know something, he should feel flattered to get that much attention."

Christina realised this was bravura, probably for Irina and Eckhart's benefit. She knew that Chuck would be on top of things and probably saving his extra identities for any necessary hurried exit from L.A.

"Any aperitifs?" Asked the waiter. They all ordered.

Then, together Bakir Jamalov and Oliver Trask arrived. Everyone made introductions. Trask had a pretty woman with him, Jamalov was alone. Sure enough Bakir and Pavle greeted each other like long lost friends.

Then it was the turn of Yaroslav Valerijovych Petruk to arrive. He greeted Jamalov and Trask in Russian. He switched to English to talk with Pavle, Eckhart and Irina, assuming they were Americans.

Christina noticed he had a smooth sounding Californian/West Coast accent when he spoke English.

Pavle called everyone to attention and explained what they would be doing. He spoke softly, in Russian and everyone nodded their agreement.

Petruk was to be the inciter of displeasure which would lead to the crashing of the deal.

The due time for Spencer came and went. They all looked uneasily at their watches. Christina hazarded that the timepieces in Wolfgang's back room were probably worth a quarter of a million dollars.

"He's always late," said Eckhart," It's in his book about how to win deals. It is supposed to make the other party feel pleased that he has even bothered to show up."

The waiter returned and asked if anyone would like to order. Irina explained that they were still waiting for the main guest to arrive.

Then, in a confusion of noise and bluster, they arrived. Kayden Lowe again, but this time, with Logan Spencer and the lawyer Myron Reinharz.

"Logan Spencer!" said Pavle, "It is great to finally meet you!" Christina worked out that Pavle's reputed wealth must have been sufficient to hold Spencer's attention. Everyone was expecting a barbed quip to fly from Spencer's mouth, but instead he seemed to be as pleasant as a sunny day.

Kayden appeared to have been given the role to growl and look like the bad cop, but really they had no idea what was coming.

"That seemed to be a generous deal you were offering back in Tokyo," Logan eventually said, "I was thinking that a Spencer Tower in the Minato City was a super idea. I had that idea myself a few months ago. Super idea."

Pavle added, "And the way that the deal is constructed there are five private investors. You, Mr Spencer, plus Saito Eiji, representing the Inagawa-kai and Minato City, plus Bakir Jamalov and Oliver Trask and then finally Yaroslav Valerijovych Petruk."

"Petruk?" queried Spencer, " I know that name? Have we met before?"

"I'm surprised you don't remember," said Petruk, "I represented the Ramenkibrava group and Salter Investments when you started that Spencer Ocean Club International Hotel and Tower in Panama."

Petruk added, "We had a deal, but you crashed the investment using Chapter 11 bankruptcy to wind everything up."

Spencer blustered, "Oh yes, it was when many projects went belly-up after the financial crisis. I had to stop Delray Beach and the Panama development."

"Yes, but with that Panama tower still an empty concrete shell, you pulled out of the project, and made Salter Investments smash dozens of buyers out of the millions of dollars they'd put down in deposits – as well as the main lender bank."

"It was little messy, but I managed to get out from under it," said Spencer, "That's why I'm looking to invest again now,"

Now Jamalov asked a question, "So is this the man who caused Salter to crash and in turn cause our construction company to lose millions of dollars because of unpaid invoices?"

"It is, " said Petruk.

"And I had been selling the completed apartments to Russian investors but had to pull from the market," announced Trask, "I was threatened with a contract on my head and that of my family until I could repay that debt."

"Sometimes business is unkind," said Kayden Lowe.

Logan Spencer looked over to Lowe, "Let me handle this please, Kayden."

Christina saw Lowe visibly shrink back into his chair.

"Put simply, I propose the deal is off," said Petruk.

"Let's not be hasty, now," said Pavle feigning support for Logan Spencer.

"No, I think Petruk is right, too many have already lost money with Mr Spencer's hollow promises and get-rich-quick schemes. We should all pull out from this," answered Jamalov.

"What about Saito EIji?" asked Oliver Trask, "Can we get him to pull out?"

"No, I believe the Inagawa-kai will want to get that Tower built and that they are simply looking for the extra funding. Saito Eiji has already told me that they could afford to build everything, but that they want to dilute their involvement. That's why they offered us all such a no-brainer.

"If Logan's in, then I'm out," said Petruk emphatically.

"Me too," said Bakir Jamalov.

"The deal is off," said Petruk.

"Maybe we should ask Mr Spencer to leave?" suggested Jamalov. He looked across the table.

"I think you'd be best to go now," said Pavle.

Kayden Lowe stood and glowered. The lawyer was also standing as if to make ready to leave the private dining area.

Logan stood, "I'll sue you all, you know," he said.

"On what grounds, there's no contract, no paper trail - nothing," said Petruk.

Spencer huffed and made his way toward the door.

Christina felt like clapping, but restrained herself.

The door slammed behind them as they left.

"Shame, I'd told the chef to expect an order of beef burger from the Spencer table," said Eckhart.

"Well, we've done it, said Irina, "we have set up Logan Spencer now, "He's going to be desperate by the time he reaches Seattle."

"Shall we order?" asked Pavle, "This is on me, they do a wonderful brigand's hat pasta, strewn with meaty honeycombs of wild morel mushrooms. At Spago, you can track the seasons through a bowl of soup."

"For entree I can suggest the steamed Virginia bass, marinated lightly in soy. It is pleasantly fleshy and moist.

"Or maybe the pan-roasted Jidori chicken? It is reliably excellent: gorgeously crisp-skinned and padded lightly with a thin, creamy layer of goat cheese.

"What about the aguachile-style octopus served in a young coconut?" asked Christina.

The waiter had returned, "It is sumptuously tender and bracingly tart," he said, "Or we do a roasted Cantonese duck which is a marvel of texture: Its sweet-sticky exterior, deliciously crisp, yields beautifully to rich, moist flesh."

"And you know, off menu we have a house-smoked salmon pizza with crème fraiche and Puck's signature Wiener Schnitzel."

"I know I'm having the Schnitzel," said Pavle.

The others became quiet as they considered the offerings.

What happened in Sydney?

It was the day of the gig, and Alex and Erebus had arrived in L.A.

Christina's first impression was that except for Alex, they all looked tired and lack-lustre.

"What's been happening?" asked Christina.

"Quite a lot," said Alex. She was talking quite rapidly.

"Erebus had a big bust-up with Darius. They worked out that he has been cheating them out of touring profits. I guess you'd call it embezzlement. He was doing it two ways. First, by re-hiring all of the equipment to the band. He'd negotiate to get it all from a local firm, then add on a mark-up and put it through his own company. His mark-up was 42%, which was enough to make some of the items look high-end when they were just regular kit."

"How was he found out?"

"Well, you remember in Tokyo, he was desperate to use the band's kit rather than the house equipment? That was what he's done for the whole of this trip and the last couple of tours. He's made a shed load of money by simply overcharging the band for everything. It came to light when something got broken and he wanted to charge the venue for a replacement. Stupidly, he used his own price-list and the venue called him out. He was charging rental that was higher than the new cost for the piece of equipment. Then the band started looking through the numbers and realised what he'd been doing."

"The second way he cheated was mainly because the band have moved to bigger venues. He was negotiating splits on the car-parking and sometimes percentages on the catering, but he was keeping it all. It turns out that a $6 hot-dog has a $1 cut built in for the artists. 20,000 hot dogs are a lot of one dollars, which were all going to his own account instead of Erebus."

"Then there was the incident on stage with the support band. Darius had brought in a replacement for Christina Nott, called GSX, who were an all-girl band, who sang tribute act songs. They all looked a lot better than they sang and part way through, the crowd seemed to be getting restless.

"Then, suddenly, a couple of men ran onto the stage. They had what looked like a fishing net. They put it over the lead singer - she was taller than the rest, knocked her to the floor and pulled her off stage like a Christmas tree in one of those - you know - those net things they use.

"Well, the band were professional enough to play on through it. I think that was because they were using a comp or a click track of drums or something, but it meant once they had started a song they couldn't really stop until the end of the clicks.

"Of course it got positioned as a great hype at the concert, 'GSX singer Sabrin kidnapped while performing live,' and so Erebus didn't really get any coverage. It was the pink mallets all over again!"

"I spoke to GSX after the concert and they were genuinely quite worried, but apparently whoever had done it had been looking for someone else. Sabrin was returned to her hotel a couple of hours after the concert. I'm just so glad it didn't happen when we were playing - that some loonies would run onto the stage and try to grab one of us. Probably a bunch of students."

"So - you can imagine, by now we're dealing with a lot of shit from all of these things. Darius has gone into self-destruct mode, and has leaked a few band secrets too. Stuff that normally stays on the road. I'll be honest some of it was quite hurtful towards me. It turns out that Marco was seeing the lead vocalist from the band they toured with last time. And it didn't stop at the end of the tour.

"I asked him about it directly, and Marco was too shamefaced to deny it. Her name is Cato and I must say she has phoned the apartment in Vancouver a couple of times, even in the last six months. Marco always said it was some kind of co-writing gig, but damn if he didn't look guilty after Darius' revelation. Come to think of it, so did the other guys.

"Wow, so what has happened to the tour?"

"Well, it's still running, the penalties to crash the gigs are too steep. It is kind of 'The show must go on.' I asked Lucas if he'd be prepared to help out with the Erebus tech and despite it all he jumped at the chance. I can't say I blame him, it is a great opportunity, and Erebus have their own roadies too."

"It could mean that Christina Nott Band is a little depleted for the LA and Seattle gigs, but I reckon Lucas will be able to handle our stuff far more easily than the rats' nest of equipment from Erebus."

"Hey you - you need to slow down a little, you've been talking rather fast."

"I'm sorry, I took some Adderall and I'm a bit wired. Raff is a gamer and usually has a small supply. Weirdly the uppers have more of a straightening effect than the downers like Xanax. The last thing I want is to be down and miserable now after all of the negative vibes I've been receiving.

'I'm saying to you, you need to power down though. You are overloaded. Trust me," said Christina. She was thinking Alex was behaving like an interrogation suspect who'd been mildly doped.

LA Music Weekly

Christina Nott is ready to become a household name.

Even if you don't like the joy of her incredibly glossy pop music, it is undeniable that this singer and her band deserve recognition on sheer talent alone.

The Banc of California Stadium was, even with the show running late, carnage: thousands of young people with flashing heart-ended mallets upending the Zippo lighter and smartphone torch traditions.

They were supposed to be here to see Erebus, but it was obvious that most of the crowd had flocked to see what weird and wonderful thing would happen in tonight's support act show.

Word had got out about the Tokyo show and the Australian show in Sydney and, despite it being rumoured that Christina Nott was not even there, the fans had still arrived. Madly, in Sydney, there had been a stage invasion and the lead singer Christina Nott was hauled away in a fishing net.

Some reports say that this was another band GSX and the singer hauled away like a wrapped Xmas tree was Sabrin from that band, but honestly, it didn't really matter and the hype had done its business.

This crowd seemed to know every word. Considering there is only one official album and it is hard to come by, I've never heard excitement quite like it from an audience: there is such pure joy coming from the fans.

Christina Nott and Jallie T knew how to be grateful for it too - they speak to the audience like TED talkers, thankful for the opportunity to share something with such lovely people.

Jallie T was a late addition to the band. Christina Nott used to tour alone mainly in Europe and it is only for this tour (Saint Petersburg, Tokyo, Sydney, LA, Seattle) that she has added Jallie T and the band to her ensemble.

So there were astonishing moments like when they asked their audience to put down the LED mallets to do a Mexican wave. They talk to them like family. Yet the screams of adoration are louder than you'll hear anywhere else.

Every song comes with a complete small choreography, every song is sung live, every performance looks like the band are having the absolute time of their lives.

Stone cold classics such as "Feel your body all over mine" and "Hey DJ" set the world alight for three minutes at a time, with glitter and spurts of flame. You re-emerge after songs such as this and wonder when you last felt so mindlessly good for such an extended period of time. The answer: probably when you heard these songs for the first time.

Play On, Christina Nott

Yet for all their ability as a group of friends who perform intricate numbers over and over again, the band also give themselves a lot of time to explore what each of them most wants to do. Ingenue Jallie T comes on and sings from her own album whilst Ellie plays the piano. Nate gets the long guitar solo he's always wanted in I Only Borrowed It.

Crazily, Raff, the drummer gets a firecracker of a rapper piece in the middle of Splitting the Diamond. "

'I am the beat constructor, splitting every structure '

And, so my friend says, it is in a crazy 11/4 time (Hey Ya, anyone?)

And still there's the flailing of the luminescent pink mallets. Apparently there a story with these too. They ordered too many in Japan and had to air-freight them over to be ready in time for the USA leg of the tour.

Trust me, you'll want one. Even at $35.

The band have previously said they want to have a dynamic that allows them to work together and apart at once and this healthy approach imbues the show with a real sense that everyone on stage is deeply satisfied with what they've presented.

But wait, we'd come to see Erebus. The friend I brought along was not a fan of Christina Nott. "It's a bit over-produced," he argued before. "I just can't get into the songs."

By the end of the night he had his favourite performer (Christina), the one he fancied the most (Jallie T) and his list of three favourite songs.

The show banged and banged and banged until it could bang no more and even then Christina Nott still had energy to spare for us. There were dark interludes – like I'm your Hitman, Babe. You could almost imagine Christina was a hitman, she sang with such menace. And I'm just not sure at all about Some of Your Stuff Ain't Normal.

I'll be truthful, I'd thought Christina Nott was some kind of manufactured pop, but now I've experienced her mainline, there is no going back.

Oh, and I've used the entire review wordcount. Erebus were quite good as well.

Rodeo Drive

The Christina Nott and the band were all sitting together in the Roosevelt.

"So where are Erebus staying?" asked Lucas.

"They are at the Motel Park on S Figueroa Street. It is very convenient for the stadium. They hired out around ten of the rooms there. Good parking for their vans," answered Alex.

"What do you think of it?" asked Lucas.

"It was clean and friendly but there are no words to compare it with Roosevelt" said Alex shaking her head, "Let's just say it is two star."

"I'm guessing that there is not a great atmosphere with Erebus at the moment?" asked Ellie. She walked over to Alex, touched her lightly on the shoulder and said, "Are you okay?"

Alex looked up, smiled, and said, "You betcha. Have you seem our review from yesterday? In the LA Music Weekly? We smashed it!"

Chuck had been quietly reading the review.

"You know something, I could be converted to this style of music you know! That was a really good show you put on last night and it has had a great write-up today. And no-one was kidnapped!"

"Chuck? Can we use that line in our reviews?" asked Alex.

"TONITE: Christina Nott Performing: 'Nobody got kidnapped.'"

"Edgy," said Chuck, smiling.

Clare looked up," So we'll be on the plane again soon, next stop Seattle."

Irina looked at Eckhart, they called across to Christina, "Can we discuss a few ideas for the business meetings we have in Seattle, maybe bring in Clare too."

"Sure," said Christina, "But I suggest we ask Chuck as well; we can use one of the little rooms here to discuss things."

"Laters, guys, We'll come up with a few extra ideas for Seattle. Home of Grunge!" said Alex, as she watched Christina, Chuck, Clare, Eckhart and Irina wander off into a side room for a meeting.

...

Irina began, "Okay, we've got things nicely positioned now. From Tokyo and Saito Eiji we have made an offer to Logan Spencer that is too good to be true. Then here in

L.A. we have killed his chances, unless he can raise a huge amount of cash.

"Now we can present him with the one man who can salvage the deal. An American billionaire. The owner of a space exploration company. Galactix.

"We had originally planned to use one of our FSB agents in Seattle as the American billionaire. Instead, I think we should consider you, Chuck, if you are prepared to do it.

"Does that mean I have to dye my hair green?" asked Chuck, "Or adopt some other form of disguise?"

"Not really," said Christina. "I think you'll just need to go Corporate Friday Casual, in your look." We can accessorise you with a very expensive watch, some expensive shoes and then you'll look the part."

"Yes, a lot of rich Americans would aspire to have a body form like yours," said Clare, looking Chuck up and down.

"Now I know what it must feel like to be a woman walking into a bar," said Chuck, "Being assessed by the male gaze - only this time its roles reversed."

"That's right, and by the way we are used to it and the requisite man-swatting!" said Christina.

"Okay, so what do I have to do?" asked Chuck.

"Well, sound American and sound rich, to begin with, like you don't care about the cost of anything, that you are used to flying around in helicopters and staying in smart hotels."

"Roger that," said Chuck. Christina started laughing, "I think we'll have to assume the helicopters are unarmed," she said.

"Oh okay, better seats, built for comfort, minibars, that sort of thing," answered Chuck.

"Yes, Now think that you own a space exploration company. It must be worth billions. You must also be worth billions. If anyone asks, you got it from shipping and as a trade intermediary."

"Got it," said Chuck, "Just like Russian Mafia,"

"Tsk, tsk," said Christina, she looked at Clare, "Shopping?"

Clare nodded, "Shopping. We've just got time before the flight. Come on Chuck. Rodeo Drive. We can even get a lift there from one of the hotel cars!"

Sure enough, outside there were standing a couple of stretched black limousines. Clare asked the driver of the first one if they would mind taking their group of three to Rodeo Drive.

"All part of the service!" he smiled and they clambered in.

"Imagine the 'after' shopping scenes from Pretty Woman," said Clare to Chuck. "Only in reverse - we get to dress you."

"Never seen it," said Chuck.

"Big mistake. Big. Huge. We have to go shopping now,"

PART THREE

Ed Adams

Seattle

The Owls are Not What They Seem

Twin Peaks

Seattle

They had landed in Seattle. Everything seemed more homely at the luggage belts. The perpetual Erebus earth tones seemed to have found a natural home. Men were wearing checked shirts. Women were wearing pretty knitted tops over jeans. There was a prevalence of outdoor camping clothing.

Clare noticed that Christina was magically wearing a green and black checked shirt over her skinny black jeans.

"How did you get changed?" she asked.

"I had this in my hand luggage and just pulled it on over my LA tee-shirt," she explained, "Here, borrow my outer coat with hood, you'll fit right in," she reached into her bag and pulled out a slim, black hooded zip-fronted coat.

"Try it on - it'll good great with shades! - Try the left pocket""

Clare tried it on and was immediately transformed.

"Rock chic," said Irina, looking at the pair of them,"You don't waste much time!"

Jallie T appeared, also 'en vogue' in gender neutral red and black plaid coat and a dark tee with a red collar, "This is what I'd almost call Vancouver street wear!" she said, "Useful to get to the hotel, but then we'll need to go large. Hey Chuck, you look a million dollars in that get-up!" she called across, to where Chuck was standing in his freshly acquired clothes.

"I'm practising," he said, "Need to get comfortable with the look."

"My tip," said Jallie T, "Stop putting things in the pockets. It messes up the line. Get a man bag or something."

"Don't say that, he'll get a tool-belt," whispered Clare.

"I heard that, " said Chuck, smiling.

A couple of teenagers had walked up to Jallie T. They were asking for selfies.

"Sure," said Jallie T, "And how about one with Christina Nott?"

"Who?" they asked,

"The fabulous musician I'm touring with," said Jallie T, "Here, together!"

Another selfie.

"Hey, and don't forget Erebus over there."

The two teenagers were overwhelmed with the number of selfie possibilities. Lucas walked forward to them and said, "Here you are. A couple of Comps. Come to our gig!"

"Smooth operator," called Clare. Lucas smiled. Christina computed that Clare and Lucas together had been a one-night kind of thing.

The luggage arrived and they were soon on yet another long bus to the hotel.

"This one is white!" said Clare, "Still with the black glass windows! Thank you Eckhart!"

Eckhart smiled back. So far the logistics had gone well, even if he had absolutely no idea about running a band on tour. He knew he had paid over the odds for everything, but it was worth it to get the professionalism he needed.

Christina and the Band hoped into the bus. Erebus were till waiting for theirs. They had somehow forced Darius to stay for the last leg of the tour but it looked as if he was making their lives as difficult a possible.

"We can't offer them a lift, we are going to a different hotel," said Alex.

"And where will the gig be?" asked Clare.

"The hotel is the Fairmont, which is a fairly traditional hotel and then the gig is at T-Mobile Park, which is only just along the road from the hotel. It is 2 miles by road or about 5 minutes away," said Eckhart, looking at his notebook. Clare looked it up on her iPhone. "It says it is a baseball park? Does that mean it is fully open-air?" she asked.

Eckhart looked at his notes, "Yes, the Seattle Mariners play baseball there, but it has hosted plenty of music concerts including Beyoncé, Pearl Jam, Foo Fighters and Green Day. Oh, and Paul McCartney back in 2013!"

"I think we'll need to crank it to 11 for this one then," said Jallie T, "Seattle's the home of Grunge, so we'll need an extra layer of dirt in the mix."

"Oh, yes, It says here that the surviving members of Nirvana have also played here...A couple of times!" added Eckhart.

"Well, this could be interesting!" said Jallie T, "Ellie and Nate, you'd better find those distortion pedals!"

"Boss DS-2 all the way," said Nate.
  "ODB-3 for me," said Ellie.

They arrived at the hotel, checked in and Christina was shown to her suite. This time it included a grand piano in the room.

"We like to give our musicians something special," explained the porter who had shown Christina to her room.

This time Irina and Eckhart were on the same floor. Irina came around to Christina's suite.

"Wow! You pop stars certainly know how to live!" said Irina.

"Live on Eckhart's project budget," said Christina, " I take it you've booked this room for the meeting?"

"Yes, it was difficult to find somewhere that Chuck could call his billionaire bunker, even here in the land of Jeff Bezos, Bill Gates and Howard Schultz."

"Okay, that's Amazon, Microsoft and - er Starbucks?" asked Christina.

"Yes, all Washington state billionaires. And now we are adding Chuck to the pile. I guess we could say he was a low numbered Microsoft employee, that accounts for about half the state's billionaires. But I think he'll prefer the quiet stealthy approach.

"Okay, so how will this work then?" asked Christina.

"First we have to convince Logan that Chuck is loaded. That he owns the Space Exploration Company."

Eckhart cut in, "That web site and those press releases from Bigsy are brilliant. He's sent us a corporate PowerPoint briefing deck as well, so we have just about everything."

"Then we need Logan to make the pitch. Eckhart will introduce it, explaining that after Trask and Jamalov dipped out, Pavle contacted Chuck as a favour. Pavle will say he felt bad about recommending two people who ultimately turned Spencer down.

"Now, Spencer has to make the request to Chuck. It will need to be for the full amount too. That is $650 million dollars, with Saito Eiji putting up the other $350 million. "

"But why would Chuck be interested in a real estate deal in downtown Tokyo?" asked Christina.

"JAXA. The Japan Aerospace Exploration Agency," explained Irina, "Chuck wants a piece of the JAXA pie."

"But I thought after the second world war the Japanese were forbidden from building up military capabilities?" asked Christina.

"Correct to a point," said Eckhart, "but Japan achieved its JAXA status while staying within the bounds of what constitutes "peaceful uses of outer space" as per the Outer Space Treaty (OST) of 1967."

"So no Star Wars for Japan, then?"

"That's right, and if Galactix were to build its Space Exploration Headquarters in downtown Tokyo, it would be assured of the right profile."

"And guess who else has corporate headquarters in that part of Tokyo?" asked Irina, "Hitachi and Mitsubishi. Both of them are big players in the JAXA consortium and have launched satellites even this year. Japan also launched the first robotic astronaut - Kirobo - which it sent to the International Space Station.

Eckhart added, "You can see that this deal would make Galactix incredibly well connected!"

"But hold on a minute," said Christina, "This isn't real, is it?"

"I know, but it sounds real doesn't it! We've just got to get Chuck prepared to tell the story."

"I can see how this gets Spencer on the hook for the new development deal, anxious to get Chuck's money into the downtown scheme."

"That's where we work the other scheme to get a hold on the money," explained Irina.

"We tell Logan Spencer that the money will come from some Galactix subsidiaries, to not draw as much attention to the deal that is being prepared.

"And don't tell me, there's five subsidiaries, and they are the ones that Kaveladze formed in Delaware and were discovered in those Panana Papers?" asked Christina

"That's right," Said Eckhart, "Namely: DUO Booster Rockets, PSR Launch Systems, HGL Weightless Cargo Winches, KNS Cosmic Navigation Systems and SZDP Wildlife Protection Frames - the makers of gecko cages!"

"I see, so we get Chuck to say he is paying for the deal from those five Russian firms, which are technically still FSB holdings? " Asked Christina.

"Right, so Galactix invests in the Minato City deal that Logan Spencer wants. It looks as if the money has come straight from a bunch of Kremlin-held accounts.

"Logan Spencer looks set to gain $180 million from that deal. Instead of two or three backers from LA, Logan Spencer has gone with one backer - Chuck - who is fronting the full investment, but split across five companies."

Irina nodded, "Right, and that's the point where our other plan kicks in. We have to make a trip to Deutsche Union Bank (Dresden). This is where Eckhart has to pose as Zakharovich. We have worked out two scenarios. There's the messy one where Eckhart extracts the money as bearer bonds, but an altogether cleaner one where the money is simply transferred to a new plausible sounding company."

"Noo," said Christina, "You wouldn't!"

"Yes we would. What could be more plausible than five space exploration companies settling a payment with a huge space exploration company - Galactix. We'll even have Chuck along for the meeting and if the bank wishes that can cross check with the Galactix bankers."

"In effect we will be pulling all of the money out of those five laundering accounts and putting it into a new company's account."

"Now the tricky bit is that we have to register the company to Logan Spencer, although the Bank account will be registered to Chuck Manners."

"I see, so Spencer gets the blame for stealing the laundered money to make his own deal work. The Kremlin will go ballistic. Spencer, in the mean time, will realise that the Minato City deal won't work. He will be receiving a taste of his own medicine."

"And we'll get the unknown quantity of money that has been cleaned through those accounts, and has been sitting in the five Russian Space companies!"

"Ideally we won't even be spotted doing any of this. Spencer will be up to his eyebrows in indebtedness to Moscow after this, which is the FSB objective achieved. We'll hopefully be up to our eyebrows in money, which is our objective achieved."

"Won't this get very dangerous though? If someone in the Kremlin realises that this has been operated from the inside. They don't forget or forgive. Ever." stated Christina.

"Agreed," said Eckhart, "But there will be nothing to link us to any of this. The Russians can hardly raise a formal complaint that someone has stolen their stolen money. That's the money that they were trying to launder."

"Okay, " said Christina, "We'll need to go through all of this again with Chuck and I think we should invite Clare to sit in to review the plan. But before all of that, we've a show to put on!"

Ed Adams

Smells like Teen Spirit

With the lights out, it's less dangerous
Here we are now, entertain us
I feel stupid and contagious
Here we are now, entertain us
A mulatto, an albino, a mosquito, my libido

Hello, hello, hello, how low
Hello, hello, hello, how low

Chris Novoselic / David Grohl / Kurt Cobain

Play On, Christina Nott

Stella shakes Seattle - my blog.

It was a fabulous venue for the Erebus concert. We were in section 123 row 31 seats 9 and 10 and the view was fantastic! Not only did we have an amazing view of the stage we could also see the Seattle skyline outside! We loved how it was open air at the top. People were friendly, and the security was quick and efficient.

Now Danny, my other half, knew just about every Erebus song by heart, and this show was a showcase for the glorious harmony singing that helped to make the Canadian band one of the world's biggest-selling groups.

While there's a steely professionalism to the Erebus, the singer Marco's address to the crowd has all the warmth of an air steward going through an in-flight safety demonstration — yet there is a tenderness to their best work.

I couldn't help noticing a few times when they seemed to be off-kilter with one another. It was as if there was something else going on between some of the members of the band. The bass was muted at times. There were a couple of what looked like angry exchanges between the drummer and the lead vocalist. Once the manager (I'm guessing) ran on stage and took over the mike during a song change.

Maybe they all have the tour jitters? I know they have a reputation for being laid back but - well - this was sometimes something else. I left the gig afterwards and tuned into twitter to see if I could make some sense of what had been occurring on stage. Nothing. Just other people like me, confused and a little deflated.

I should mention the support band.

Christina Nott. They seemed to come from an entirely different planet than Erebus. It was odd to see the two bands sharing the same stage. I was told that fans of this band come along in small armies with glow-sticks and holding up smartphone torches. No-one prepared me for the neon mallets. These heart-shaped pink gavels were on sale everywhere. Outside the stadium they were on-sale for $20 and inside they were all of $30.

Well they made the whole gig look insane, with Christina Nott strutting the stage with her small but loud band playing her top tunes. Quite varied they were too, and a couple of them were real ear-worms. Christina explained that the band had brought along extra pedals to help create a special Seattle vibe to the tunes.

This got a huge cheer and then Nate, the guitarist played the opening chords of 'Smells like Teen Spirit'. This got an even bigger cheer and then Christina Nott and Jallie T came on with Pom Poms like in the Nirvana video and sang the whole song. And someone apparently called Lucas was cleaning the right side of the stage with a mop - like that guy in the video. So cool. The whole of Seattle stopped for two-and-a-half-minutes. Unforgettable.

Later they played an anthem 'This one's for the FANS' and it has really stuck with me since the gig. I've sought her album afterwards, which I was warned was difficult to obtain in an American imprint.

You know something, I love the album. I'm embarrassed to say I think I enjoyed the support more than the main act this time. Sorry Erebus. Sorry Danny.

This room ain't big enough for the both of us

Irina and Eckhart looked at Christina's room. The suite for the meeting. It was light coloured, very pleasant and airy. It contained a grand Piano.

"I'm sorry, but this just isn't big enough," said Irina. Christina nodded, "I was thinking the same thing. With two big egos in the room, we'll need somewhere bigger or somewhere exclusive."

"You know what? How about the Space Needle? We could book out a corner spot?" said Irina.

Christina nodded, "That's a good idea. We could have a round table, separated from others and there would be a great skyline talking point."

"The nature of the place means we don't have to worry about it being tip top billionaire territory either," said Eckhart.

Christina added, "It gets around the problem that by reputation Logan Spencer is a fussy eater too. We can pretty much get anything in the Needle. The line of sight is good if anyone wants to try anything unusual, too."

Chuck arrived.

"We are thinking of moving venue," said Eckhart, "This room isn't big enough."

"I was thinking the same thing," said Chuck, in another crisp light blue shirt, that showed off his tanned arms.

"We need something sparkly around your wrist. To make you look more expensive," said Irina.

"Here," she said, she reached into her bag and found a chunky silver bracelet.

"Try it," she urged, as Chuck looked a little uncertain.

"And that watch will have to go," you'll be better to not have one at all.

"Show them you are free-spirited."

He put on the bracelet.

"Mmm," murmured Eckhart, "That make you instantly look more expensive. But not in a bling way. You'd need another two or three pieces for that."

"I've read the notes about Galactix and the basics of how we intend to move this forward. I need to finally cave in to Logan Spencer's request to provide the funding. $600 million? Am I on the right track?"

"Yes, Chuck, that should do fine," answered Christina, "And remember we'll all be there to help steer the conversation along."

"One more thing, asked Chuck, "Why would Christina, Irina and Eckhart be at this meeting as well as the ones in Tokyo and L.A.?"

"They are the representatives for 'the deal' Eckhart is the contract man, Christina is security and I am Corporate Oversight," explained Irina.

"Oh, Okay, I wanted to make sure it made sense," said Chuck, "But should I have someone along as well? - Like a lawyer or something?"

"That's a good point," said Irina, "I think we could bring Clare as backup, but I think you'd be better to show up alone and suggest that your people will handle things afterwards. In an emergency you could bring Clare into the discussion, but it would be better if you didn't need her."

"Okay, we'll go with that plan, then."

Eckhart had already called the Spencer organisation and rescheduled the meeting point. He explained it would be a better place to get a fantastic view across the city.

Seattle Space Needle

Seven o'clock.

"I forget that you Americans all eat early," said Christina.

They were sitting at a large round table in the Space Needle.

"The view all around was spectacular. They could see the sea of Puget Sound and there was a giddying view down toward the ground.

"We've less late arrivals to worry about this time, " said Christina, looking towards the door.

A few minutes passed and then one of Spencer's bodyguards arrived. He looked indifferent to his role, as if to say, there would be no trouble.

In walked Spencer. He looked around at everyone. Behind him was Hayden Lowe and a new person, who Christina assumed was a lawyer.

"Hello Mr Spencer," said Irina, " Let me introduce you to everyone,"

Spencer ignored Irina but spotted Chuck and incorrectly said, "Hi, you must be Chuck DesChamps,"

"That's right, I'm Chuck Desjardins and these are my colleagues, Irina Morozova, Eckhart Bloch and Christina Nott. Irina and Eckhart are business advisors for the deal. We've all read your papers that you sent on ahead."

Spencer continued to ignore everyone except Chuck.

"So what do you know about this opportunity?" asked Spencer.

"Well Pavle Darchidze contacted me about it. We're both members of Bill's - it's a little club for a few of us businessmen here in Washington. We meet over at Snoqualmie Falls."

"Bill's?" asked Spencer blankly.

"Yes it was one of the member's little jokes - It stands for Billionaires of course. The other rule says, "If you have to ask how much it costs to join, then you can't come in."

"Well, so Pavle was telling me because he knew I was interested in some Tokyo property. To do with my Space Exploration interests. I guess you've seen the web-site?"

"I've seen some pictures," said Spencer.

"Well, I want to get hooked in with that JAXA, The Japan Aerospace Exploration Agency, and this could be a fast track. I'd want Galactix in big letters on the outside of the building, in what is a prime spot in downtown Minato City. A couple of my big suppliers operate from Minato.

Hitachi and Mitsubishi both have corporate offices there."

"Well, this is the situation," said Spencer, realising that the Minato opportunity could be even bigger than he thought, "I've got the lead investor on-side and they are looking for additional funding. It was to go to a couple of other investors, but I discovered that they were unsuitable."

Christina marvelled at how Spencer was bending the truth. The other investors had backed out.

"So how much will I need to be in with this scheme, then?" asked Chuck.

"It will amount to some $650 million, which will secure you the best offices and external Naming Rights, alongside my Spencer branding."

"Woah, Whats that? I didn't know this was to be a co-branded development? I'd imagined it to be something like Galactix Tower or something similar, so that Japanese would see I was serious!" Chuck folded his arms and started to look as if he would disengage.

"Just a moment, I think I we can work this out. How about we change the Naming Rights clause? It could be something like "Galactix Tower, developed by Spencer Holdings."

"That sounds more like it, and I'll get the Naming Rights on local Infrastructure too?" It would be cool to have Galactix Boulevard and a couple of other smaller streets named after my kids!"

Spencer looked across to his lawyer - he was nodding.

"They seem like perfectly reasonable requests."

"Okay, well we'll have to consider how we can make the down payments for this scheme. Now call me old fashioned, but I quite like what Walt Disney did when he was buying Disneyworld. Instead of one big purchase, he split it up into lots of tiny parcels of land."

"That's what I'm thinking I'll do. Not dozens, but maybe just five or six of my space subsidiaries. I'll move the money from Galactix to your account, but it will be from several smaller companies.

Heck - you give me the account number where you want the money and I'll start the wheels in motion. You can imagine it will take a while to liquidate £650 million and parcel it into small pieces. And we'll still need to discuss the actual phasing, but I'm assuming that around $200 million would be the right first phase payment?"

Spencer nodded. He could not believe his luck. Chuck DesJardins was either very trusting or very stupid.

Chuck continued, "These are the companies we'll use and today I'll rely on a handshake, ahead of the legal papers which could take weeks to come through. You don't mind if I ask Christina there to take a photograph of us signing? It's not for the press. Just so we have something on file.

Christina picked up her phone and Chuck and Logan shook hands holding up the paperwork.

"Wow, you are very relaxed and a little unconventional about this," said Logan.

"Put it this way, I remember everyone alive that has ever tried to cross me," said Chuck, "And that is quite easy because there are not many of them living." He laughed at this and Logan could not work out whether he was serious.

Chuck continued, "You should get the payments from DUO Booster Rockets, PSR Launch Systems, HGL Weightless Cargo Winches, KNS Cosmic Navigation Systems and SZDP Wildlife Protection Frames. Expect the first payments to be small whilst we vet the financial systems and then I'll release the rest of the money in ever-increasing lots."

Spencer looked taken aback. "I'm slightly surprised that we've concluded this so quickly."

"Look, I know your reputation Mr Logan Spencer. You don't seem to know mine, but where I come from if you grab enough land, something good is bound to come from it."

"Are there any other points to run through?" asked Spencer to his still un-introduced lawyer.

"No these information packs seem to cover just about everything," said the lawyer, gesturing to the neatly prepared bound sets of papers that had been laid out on the table.

"Well, in that case, maybe I should be bidding you farewell," said Chuck, standing. The bracelet on his arm caught the light, " I have a plane to catch shortly, I know it's my own jet, but I don't like to keep them waiting. You know something though, I got a deal on that from Boeing, through Bill's - we should probably call it Bill's discount club."

Chuck laughed, slapped Logan Spencer on the back and ushered him towards the exit from the restaurant.

Christina listened for the ping of the arriving elevator and then again when it was down at ground level.

Only then did they all laugh and applaud Chuck, who quietly took a lap around the table, with his arms out like wings.

Clare walked across from another table.

"Judging from the body language, that went pretty well!" she asked.

"Oh yes, better than you could imagine," said Irina, "Chuck is a born actor,"

Eckhart solemnly nodded in agreement. "Chuck, you were fantastic. I was expecting the deal to crash when you started arguing about name-boards or something!"

Chuck smiled, "I thought I'd argue about something involving his ego, and something we could ultimately let him win. It makes the deal more satisfying from his perspective."

Irina looked serious, "Okay, now we need to move quickly. We must make Logan Spencer appear to be a Director of Galactix and then it can look as if Logan was siphoning the money from the Russian companies to his own account."

She pause, then added, "Alongside that, we need Eckhart to visit the Deutsche Union Bank (Dresden) posing as Zakharovich. Then he can transfer the funds from the five companies to the Galactix bank account, except the Galactix bank account in Switzerland will be run by us."

Clare added, "I see, so anyone following the audit trail will see the five companies paying Galactix up to $650 million, all in small pieces. They will also see that Logan Spencer is the main director of Galactix. Neat!"

Irina continued to look serious, "The Kremlin will want to explode at this news, but can't make it public because of the money laundering scandal, which could affect their entire political administration.

"Instead, they are very likely to lean hard on Logan Spencer. That is exactly what our primary mission required."

"Okay, but what about all of that unaccounted money?" asked Chuck, "Where is that going?"

"Expenses for us," said Christina, "I'm in with Eckhart and Irina for a one third share,"

Chuck nodded, "I see the ill gotten gains get rehoused!"

Irina interrupted, "We'd talked about this. If the money is anywhere close to $200 million, let alone $600 million, then it is far more than we had expected. Honestly, we were thinking a few million apiece. Eckhart and I decided that we should split the money five ways instead of three. That's us, Christina, Chuck and you, Clare as a thank you for the way your team have helped us through this."

"Agreed, " said Christina, "I was about to ask you the same thing!"

Chuck and Clare smiled at this. It wasn't the first time that either of them had re-housed dubious funds.

"Tomorrow we need to move fast," said Eckhart. The nearest Deutsche Union Bank is across the US in New York. I'll fly there tomorrow and initiate the transfers. Chuck, it will be so much better if you come along in person to represent Galactix before we sack you as a director!"

"Count me in, " said Chuck, "I'll be ready for the first flight in the morning."

"Thats around 7.40 am, said Irina, Delta flight. Gets in at around 4 pm - to JFK."

"That's fine, I'll get that one unless they are full," said Chuck. Eckhart, I guess you are already booked?"

"Yes," said Eckhart, "although I can't remember the exact flight. But leave things with me and I'll get us hotel rooms and a pickup from the airport as well."

"I'll come along too," said Christina, "A little extra assistance, and it's a while since I was in The Big Apple."

Irina added, "Its all agreed then, Eckhart, Chuck and Christina to New York tomorrow!"

Eckhart said, "You know what, we should really order some food, this restaurant looks like it could be fun"

"I'm having a burger," said Chuck, "A Spencer Special."

New York State of Mind

I was sleeping, gently napping, when I heard the phone
Who is on the other end talking, am I even home
Did you see what she did to him, did you hear what they said
Just a New York conversation, rattling in my head

Oh, my, and what shall we wear
Oh, my, and who really cares

Lou Reed

New York, New York

Eckhart had arranged a stretch limo from JFK, and the man was standing outside the Arrivals gate holding an iPad with Hr. Bloch displayed on it. They followed the liveried man from the gate to where his car was part and Christina let out a stifled laugh when she saw the vehicle. It was similar to the ones in L.A., but somehow longer and more bling-filled. It also looked as if it had a past. A long past down seedy alleyways visiting dubious clubs.

Then clambered in and were surrounded by strips of LED lights flashing in multiple colours.

"Big Box, Little Box," said Christina, imitating a dance move. Eckhart, normally serious, laughed at this. "Welcome to New York" he said.

Christina's phone was bleeping and had been doing so crazily since she had left the plane. Now she was seated she decided to see what all of the fuss was about.

"They are mostly from Bigsy," she said, "He's found someone has been monitoring our LAN back in London. Something about CIPAV monitoring from the CIA?"

"CIPAV is something that the FBI use," said Chuck, "It's one of those Trojan Horses designed to read all of your traffic."

"What all of the messages?" said Christina, "Not exactly, but it knows where you have linked to. There's too much home security legislation to allow for a direct wiretap like that."

"At least that's what they tell you, " said Christina, "I don't think Russia would be quite so picky."

"Yes, I've often wondered if it is a ruse, " said Chuck, "They say that the Antivirus companies have all agreed to not identify CIPAV and Magic Lantern when they are installed on a computer. That gives the FBI an immense advantage. They can pretty well re-write the viruses and still no-one would know. To tell the truth, I'm amazed that Bigsy has found them in your LAN."

"Bigsy has strange powers," said Christina, "And knows quite a few hackers."

"I think you need to nowadays," said Chuck, " I remember when the then-FBI director James Comey defended a sting where FBI agents fabricated an Associated Press news story and the impersonation of an AP reporter by an FBI agent."

He paused as is thinking about how much to say. Christina worked out that Chuck had been involved.

"They were trying to locate a kid who was calling out bomb threats all over the place and hooked him with a fake email that had some kind of payload. The story was that they used CIPAV, but I think that was just put out there.

"Comey then wrote a letter to the editorial Board of the New York Times: 'To Catch a Crook, The FBI's Use of Deception,' Of course, the Freedom of the Press gang got onto the First Amendment, so the use of these tools by the Government been somewhat cloaked in mystery ever since."

"It's a kind of madness though," said Christina, "Russia will extract everything it can from a target. Remember those emails from Hillary's office? Oh yes, I should say allegedly."

Chuck and Eckhart nodded and then looked towards the skyline. 'Welcome to the Big Apple' said a high sign on the side of a building by the elevated roadside.

"So where are we all staying?" asked Christina, "looking to Eckhart."

"I've gone for central, but small rooms. I thought we are only here for one night and are already luxuried-out. We are staying at the W on Times Square."

"Perfect," said Christina, "I've actually stayed there before. The check-in is on the eighth floor."

"Then, shall we hit it?" asked Christina, "The town I mean?"

She realised˙ that Irina and Eckhart looked zoned out from the travel. Chuck was smiling though. "Come on then, you'll need to wear some of those fancy clothes we got you in Rodeo Drive if you are coming out with me!" she said. She noticed Chuck was looking around the lobby. He smiled, "I'm on it!" he said.

MOMA Nights

"So where shall we go?" asked Christina, They were sitting in the lobby of the hotel.

"This is your continent, Chuck!"

"Yes, but I have a feeling you know New York as well as I do!" said Chuck. He waved two tickets in front of Christina.

"From the concierge. MOMA Nights! I've got us tickets to the cocktail evening at MOMA.

"But first, in keeping with Christina Nott, I suggest we head over to Serendipity III."

"Oh, Chuck, I've always wanted to go there," said Christina, "To try one of those Frrrozen Hot Chocolates; I'm told it can bring out the child in anyone!"

"The concierge told me he'd book us a table there too. He was explaining that it is the place where artists got their inspiration and actors fulfilled their cravings. Marilyn

Monroe, Andy Warhol, Grace Kelly and Cary Grant then continuing with Cher, Candice Bergen, Melanie Griffith right up to Beyoncé, Selena Gomez and Kim Kardashian."

Christina added, "Yes, apparently the original owners (the three IIIs of the name) arrived as teenagers and met at a dance class. The three princes of Serendip opened the first themed restaurant for comfort food and everything was for sale, including the Tiffany Lamps and marble tables they found and installed. We'll eat ice cream and then have cocktails? An interesting experiment!"

"That's what the concierge said, but he wasn't sure that we'd get into Serendipity later. The Museum of Modern Art is open until late."

"Look - there's a second reason for going to Serendipity," added Chuck speaking quietly.

"I think you are being followed, don't look around but the two over there are the puffin and auks of the CIA."

He nodded into a corner where a man and woman were sitting talking to one another. The woman was wearing a headset, but it looked like an iPhone EarPods that she had forgotten to remove.

"It's a case of 'it takes one to know one,'" said Chuck. "They are so obviously agents kitted out in the regulation way. I wouldn't be surprised to see little stars and stripes flags in their lapels."

"But I want to make it easy for them to follow us to Serendipity, I'm going to loudly discuss it when we walk over past that table."

"I bet you can't get them into the same elevator as us!" jested Christina.

Sure enough, they walked over to the table where the two were sitting.

"Yes, Serendipity 3; it's at 225 E 60th Street, it's about a couple of miles. It should take around 15 minutes in a yellow cab," said Chuck to Christina, "Once we are back at ground level!"

They caught the elevator. It was just closing when Chuck placed his boot in the door.

"Hi, I thought I'd be neighbourly," he said. The two agents sheepishly got into the same elevator and they all travelled to the ground. Christina was talking about the ice creams the entire time.

Outside, it was like an end of the world daylight apocalypse. There was so much neon and LED light pulsing. A large and rather pointless store proclaimed M&Ms. There were illuminated movie posters the size of a row of houses.

"Yes, I know, you do sort of forget."

They hailed a cab and were soon outside Serendipity. "Stand by the door," said Christina, "I'll take a photo of you where Andy Warhol sat!"

They entered the small but deep restaurant and a very actorish waiter showed them to a small square table which could seat four.

"This is going to be fun!" said Christina, "And look who have just walked in." It was the two tails from the W Hotel.

They could see the waiter shaking his head. They had not booked and would need to make a reservation for another day. Chuck stood and walked over to the waiter.

"No, actually these are our friends from the hotel. They can certainly share our table."

The waiter looked around, he knew there was something not right, but Christina smiled such a lovely smile back towards him.

"Oh, I don't know what you are up to, but party on," said the waiter and showed all three of them back to the table where Christina was sitting.

"You two were the people we shared an elevator with," started Chuck, "Back at the W?"

"Oh yes," said the woman, "I thought I recognised you from somewhere."

"So why are you following my friend here?" asked Chuck directly.

"C'mon guys, you have CIA written all over your faces, your manner. Who is your director? I expect I know him?"

The two agents looked at one another.

"Busted," said Chuck, "You are both busted, just admit it, before I need to spring the real trap in here."

Christina knew Chuck was bluffing, but he spoke with such an ominous tone even she was thinking the restaurant had been staked out.

The woman looked at the man and nodded. "Yes, all right, we have been asked to track your friend Christina Nott here. You almost threw us off the track when you booked those flights from Seattle to JFK - we were convinced they were dummies."

"Anyway, we were called in at the last moment to follow you from the airport and keep eyes on you until we could ask Christina a few questions, here in New York."

"Were you going to pull Christina from her hotel room?"

"Tonight, when she returns, someone wants to ask her some questions,"

"About what?"

"Don't know, our only part is to keep eyes on."

"Well, we think we know what it is about," said Chuck, "It's about some intel received in London. The intel was wrong."

"Go on," said the man.

"Okay, but I'd better get your name??" asked Chuck.

"I'm John Smith and this is Janet Brown," said the man.

"Ha-Ha, of course you are, " said Chuck, "Well, you don't look as if you recognise me?"

"No," said John, "We have you as a well-off playboy, American, maybe from Texas?"

"They worked, "said Chuck to Christina, "The clothes I mean,"

Christina smiled. She was holding a Sig P320 in her right hand under the table.

"Okay, well my name is Colonel Chuck Manners. I'm an agent as well. I've been a Marine and know most of the directorate at the big house. Check me out after this is over. We know you think Christina has some information from Minerva. That is a listening station in London. One that was supposed to be run by the CIA, but was subcontracted out - you will love this - to the FSB.

"They ran sleaze on British Members of Parliament and other significant players. Honey traps, financials - that sort of thing. It was a cheap way of lobbying. We only know about Bernard Driscoll, who was killed in a car accident. Christina was not involved in any of this. She happened to save me from a couple of hit-men in Brussels. That was her main link to me and to the Minerva situation."

"Ask them if they are getting all this?" Chuck looked at the woman.

Janet nodded, "Yes, they can hear loud and clear - they are fact-checking right now."

"Good and they know you are both in danger sitting here with me unless they stand down the operation?" asked Chuck, "By which I mean the follow and abduct Christina Nott."

"There's someone wants to talk to you," said Janet, "Here." She passed across a bluetooth earpiece.

"Chuck?" came a voice, it was a woman. "It's Madeleine Harris."

"Madeleine?" asked Chuck, "Remember Turkey?"

"Istanbul and that earthquake? How could I forget, when we were all evacuated onto the Hotel's lawn."

Christina was impressed. Chuck was validating that it was really Madeleine, and all by way of a pleasant conversation.

"You heard all of that, I take it?" asked Chuck. "Christina is not involved in the setup of the Minerva thing. She saved me in Brussels from those FSB assassins. The whole CIA London listening station thing is a farce if you ask me."

"Complicated times, that thing in London. But look, I'm standing down this mission" said Madeleine," The mission to seize Christina. I'm satisfied," she said, "New York? You'll have to drop by to see me the next time you are in the East."

"I'm a little shy," said Chuck, "As you know only too well!"

"Janet, did you get all of that?" asked Madeleine.

"Yes , Ma'am," replied Janet,

Christina had her head craned towards Chuck's earpiece and had heard most of what had happened.

"Mission stood down?" she asked," In an ice cream shop! All my lucky days are rolled into one."

"Okay," said Chuck, "You can put that pistol away now, Christina. Janet and John, how would you like some ice cream? I hear it is lovely here."

Fulton Street

Chuck, Eckhart and Christina were coming out of the Fulton Street subway. They were in the bustle of the New York Financial district, with a mix of tourists and business people going about their day.

Chuck was wearing a suit, which made him look like a dapper banker, maybe one with a finger in too many deals. Eckhart had another variation of long leather jacket, blue shirt and tie and Christina had decided to go Dolce and Gabbana suit.

"It will keep them off balance. The men and the women will look at me instead of you two shifty hombres," she said.

Chuck and Eckhart had to agree. Everyone was looking at Christina on the subway like she was a rare and intriguing creature. She had pulled her hair back behind her ears too, which gave her an androgynous quality.

"Shapeshifter," whispered Chuck.

"Why thank you, Sir" she returned in a Southern Belle voice.

They arrived at the corner of the Federal Reserve building and could see the tall white building ahead.

"That's where the Deutsche Union Bank has its American headquarters," said Eckhart, "Nassau Street,"

"Which leads directly to Wall Street!" said Chuck "We can't get much more Financial District than this!"

"This is a great area to talk about big numbers, too, they will be used to it," said Christina.

Eckhart was carrying a briefcase filled with documentation. He was taking no chances about the things they could be asked.

"I'm surprised that Spencer hasn't built one of his towers around here?" said Christina.

"Oh, he has, right on Wall Street by the Station. There's even a shop built into it: Rich Boy's Toys. They can sell you a life-sized Batmobile."

"Says it all, " said Christina.

Deutsch Union Bank

Inside the Bank, they had stepped from New York back into quietly opulent Germany. A black-suited woman walked quietly up to them, double checked Christina's look and then asked,

"Welcome to Deutsche Union Bank, are you here to see someone?"

Eckhart replied, Christina noticed immediately that his speech pattern had reverted to a more clipped Germanic form of English.

"Yes, we are here to see Mr Stephan Heldmann, we have an appointment for 10 o'clock. Our names are Desjardins, Zakharovich and Nott.

The woman called through on her mobile house phone and spoke quietly to someone.

"Yes, it is about Galactix. You are expected, Please follow me. We are going to the 33rd floor."

They stepped into an elevator and the woman pressed the button.

"This is the express elevator to the higher floors," she said.

In a moment they were there, and they stepped out into a light-bathed corridor and followed the woman towards a series of opulent-looking conference rooms.

"You are in Hannover," she said, "My home town actually."

They walked into the room marked Hannover and saw a long table, a projector screen and some light refreshments had been set up.

"Herr Heldmann will be with you soon, please help yourself to the refreshments and you can contact me again by pressing 9. My name is Helga."

She left a business card on the table with her details and they all sat down untidily around the table. The next half hour would be crucial.

"Ahah, and welcome to Deutsche Union Bank," said Herr Heldmann as he entered the room. He was well-dressed, sharp-looking and Christina judged him to be mid-thirties. She could see his wedding ring band. He didn't have a trace of a European accent, Christina thought he must be from New York.

They introduced themselves and Christina once more noticed Heldmann giving her a more than cursory examination. The D&G was doing its job.

"So Mr Zakharovich, may I call you Filippov ? You contacted the bank a few days go about moving some funds from several smaller companies into a larger Galactix account?"

Eckhart shifted in the chair, "Most people call me Vova, actually, it's a Russian thing you know,"

"Oh, I'm sorry, Vova, is that better? I hope we can all get along."

"And Mr Desjardins, Chuck? I believe you are the CEO of Galactix? That's a pretty large private company."

"Yes, we are quietly consolidating our assets at the moment," explained Chuck, "We have some new business in Japan and it will be better for us if we have ready access to certain funds."

"Okay, you'd better stop there, or we'll all be up for insider trading. I should have mentioned that these rooms record the conversations - purely for audit purposes."

"That's okay, we are used to being spied upon, " joked Chuck.

"Well, here are the various accounts, I think you needed to verify that I was an authorised signatory and that so is Mr Desjardins. I have brought both of our passports as further identification," said Eckhart, still posing as Zakharovich.

Then, we'll fire up a computer and can make the transfers. We have Ms Nott as our legal representative. Will you need to bring in someone else as well?"

"I doubt that will be necessary," said Stephan, "we have automated audit on the computer screens, plus the recording in the room. Sometimes when the sums get larger, we might need to bring someone in."

Stephan took the passports and examined them.

"Great. I'll take copies of the identity pages, if I may. Now we'll bring up the accounts. We start with the 'From:' accounts - there should be five and then the 'To:' account there should just be one. Thank goodness we have all of the numbers for the accounts, My Russian is not up to the task.

He started to type in the reference numbers and soon had the five accounts listed.

"So how much are you transferring from each account?"

"All of the reserves," said Eckhart, "As I said, we are consolidating them into the new account."

"Well, it is an intra-bank transfer too, although I notice you have set up the Galactix account in Switzerland."

"Yes, to be truthful we wanted to have simple multiple currency access, and we somehow thought the Swiss were very good at that."

"Well it pains me to see the money leave the New York Branch, but at least it will still be in our Bank," said Stephan.

Right, let's see what we have on balance...

- двигательные установки ограничены - DUO Booster Rockets $177,234,594.80
- пусковые системы россии - PSR Launch Systems $132,543,764.80

- невесомые грузовые лебедки - HGL Weightless Cargo Winches $234,967,456.76
- космические навигационные системы - KNS Cosmic Navigation Systems $482,376,738.65
- Средства защиты дикой природы - SZDP Wildlife Protection Frames $117,456,875.78

Let's see now:

$$177,234,594.80$$
$$132,543,764.80$$
$$234,967,456.76$$
$$482,376,738.65$$
$$117,456,875.78$$
$$1,144,579,430.79$$

"Ah, $1.14 billion. That is a little more than I was expecting. Maybe I will need to have someone else in the room to witness the transfer."

He picked up a phone similar to the one that Helga had carried.

"Helga, can you come over here a minute, I need you to witness an intra-bank transfer of funds."

A moment later Helga re-entered the room. She once more glanced toward the detail of Christina's suit and then turned to Stephan.

"Look, we are helping Mr Zakharovich consolidate the funds for Galactix. They want to have them ready for something in Tokyo.

Eckhart/Zakharovich coughed loudly.

"Oh, I am sorry, that last remark was confidential," said Stephan.

"Have you checked the passport ids?" asked Helga, quite business-like.

"Yes, and cross checked the check digits of the accounts," said Stephan, "We are good to go once you have added your authorisation code."

Helga walked to the terminal and typed in a long string of codes.

Then Stephan picked a small unit from his pocket, typed some numbers and received back a passkey.

"We have to use these double authentication systems nowadays," he said, "it is to prevent fraud."

He typed in the last digit and pressed enter.

"There," he said, "All done. Let me refresh the screens."

He pressed enter again and the five accounts all showed a zero balance.

The once - empty account in Switzerland now showed a healthy balance. $ 1,144,539,530.79.

"That should be the new amount minus our handling fee."

"It looks correct according to our calculations," said Zakharovich.

"Excellent," said Chuck and rose to shake Stephan's hand, "now I'm off to take a look at some artwork," he said, "I visited the MOMA last night and it has put me in the mood to get some modern art related to space travel."

"Kabakov," said Helga, "Ilya Kabakov - he's a Russian artist who has made several installations about space and time. Try looking for ' The man who flew into space from his apartment' or 'How to meet an angel.' They are both terrific."

"Thank you for that, Helga, I'll take a look for both."

"I studied modern European Art at college."

"Okay, well seeing as our business is concluded, we should really be making a move now," said Chuck, standing.

Helga said, "Yes, let me take you back to the elevators,"

"Yes, It's a long way down," said Chuck, saying quoting one of Christina's songs which he had learnt over the concert tour.

Pier 17

"We are so close to Pier 17 it would seem a shame not to visit," said Christina, as they turned the corner into Water Street. Each of them was looking around, carrying out basic surveillance to ensure they were not being followed when they left Deutsche Union Bank.

"Agreed," said Chuck, and they set off along busy streets towards Fulton.

Then onto the Pier, where they soon found a suitable large restaurant area, with a good view back towards the whole Financial District.

Only when they were seated, did Christina say, "Whew - I think we did it!" Eckhart smiled, "Yes I think we now have a huge amount of money in the Swiss subsidiary of Deutsche Union Bank. The money is clean so I think we need to write some healthy invoices to get it transferred quickly to other accounts."

Christina nodded, she was no stranger to needing to squirrel money away and she was sure that Chuck was the same. Come to think of it, Chuck had once carried a huge stash of banknotes around in a rucksack.

Indeed, Christina was most concerned about Eckhart and Irina who had little experience of handling such large sums.

"I had no idea," said Eckhart, "That the sums would be so huge."

"Me neither," said Chuck, "You made it look as if it was going to be $200k tops."

"It gives us a pressing problem to move the money quickly, before someone at the Russian end of things discovers something."

"Even if they do, we should be in the clear," said Christina, "The company that appeared to 'steal' the money is owned by Logan Spencer. Come to think of it, I'd better ask Bigsy to remove Chuck from the company web-site."

She paused and tapped a short request into her phone. An almost immediate response came back from Bigsy. "Already done. We saw the money move. Spectacular :-)"

"He's already moved you out of the company, Chuck Desjardins. It was useful that you still had your Canadian Passport to muddy the water still further. Can I call Jake now? He will know what to do to shunt the money away from prying eyes."

They both looked at Eckhart, who was clearly out of his depth.

"Look Eckhart, you and Irina are both sitting on more than a quarter of a billion dollars. Between the two of you that is half a billion. You'll need to have a system to protect it."

"I know, it is almost too much. I'm not sure how I can even tell Irina about this. We were both hoping for maybe two or three million dollars from our scam."

Christina nodded, "It illustrates how much money is in play. These are serious amounts. Both Chuck and I are already 'three-flagged', you know, we have citizenship in one jurisdiction, residence in another and a business base in a third. I've got a slew of passports, Icelandic, Russian, British, Dutch. I'm pretty sure Chuck also has a matching set of United States, Canadian and Swiss passports. You'll need to get something similar, as well as setting up companies in tax havens."

"Can we be caught?" asked Eckhart.

"Not at all," said Christina, "You've heard of the old school tie? Well one of the things that all those British schoolboys learn is how to keep money. Money and Power. Look at any of their politicians, they will have money stashed all over the place. Just like it showed in those Panama Papers - and when they were discovered even the Prime Minister David Cameron's father was named for having offshore accounts."

"Now it is my turn to look in a small notebook : An archaic example - Jacob Rees-Mogg - As per the Independent Parliamentary Standards Authority (IPSA), his salary as an MP was £76,011 yet his lifestyle is altogether more loaded Aside from a selection of vintage cars he also owns a £5m million property behind Westminster Abbey, the £4m freehold of a building in

Pall Mall and the £1.5m leasehold of a flat inside it. In 2007, he founded Somerset Capital Management. He stepped back from the running of it when he became an MP, but retained an advisory role, which he later withdrew from in 2019 following his appointment as the Leader of the House of Commons. Some could say it was hypocritical when SCM moved its centre of operations to Ireland as part of Brexit-proofing.

"Or take the one-time austerity Chancellor of the Exchequer in Britain, George Osborne. He only has a wealth of around £4 million, but part of that is through a tax-efficient trust fund which covers his 15% stake in the company Osborne and Little. He can also fall back on Irish residency, with his Irish baronetcy.

"Then there is that pleasant man Rishi Sunak, allegedly the richest man in the UK cabinet. He worked in the hedge fund sector and eventually launched his own firm called Theleme Partners in 2010. Notice any themes around trust funds?

"In his role as Chancellor, Mr Sunak's salary is £71k, which excludes his salary as an MP which is £79k. However, Mr Sunak is married to Akshata Murthy, the daughter of Indian billionaire and consultancy firm owner of Infosys, N. R. Narayanan Murthy, who is worth an estimated £1.99bn according to Forbes."

"You've spent too long in London, quoting everything in GBP," said Chuck, smiling.

Christina continued, "Maybe, Chuck, but you see, Eckhart, you'll need some back story to go with the wealth, but the school tie owners will want to make it easy for you, at least in some jurisdictions."

Eckhart nodded. This was all new to him.

"My advice though? However much you love the Motherland, keep the money away from it. I've seen too many monied Russians ultimately hunted down for their wealth. Especially the new guard hunting the old guard, apparently with the Kremlin's blessing."

Christina dialled through to Jake.

"Hi Jake, I think we'll need to move that money soon. Away from prying eyes. I know, it was a lot. To be honest, none of us realised how much. A couple of minutes and I'll ask him"

"Chuck, Jake wants to know if we can transfer your money to your usual consultancy account? You'll need to issue an invoice for something though."

"I'd forgotten you had my account. Yes, send it to the Swiss Bank for the moment. It can go against Project Petrograd."

"I don't know if you could hear that, Jake, Chuck would like his fifth of the total to go to his usual account - that's the Swiss one - and against a project called Project Petrograd."

"You'll know how to process my share and the fifth that is going to The Triangle? Yes, that's right. Like we usually do. Exactly."

"The rest? The other 40%? I don't think they have worked it out yet. Maybe you could just move it temporarily to somewhere else? - What? You'll check with Bigsy. Okay. That's fine. I'll tell them. Yes it is lovely here. Hot. We are outside looking over the East River. Where? Pier 17.

"I know, it's great. Oh yes, we were being followed but had an interesting encounter in the ice cream shop, when they suddenly decided to cease and desist! See you! "

Christina clicked to end the call.

"All being done. Jake is moving Chuck's and my money out into our accounts. The Triangle money is also being moved. Both Eckhart's and Irina's money will also be moved away from Galactix, but I don't know where at the moment. Bigsy and Jake are getting their heads together.

Christina noticed Eckhart still looked troubled.

"Don't worry, though, Eckhart, your money is much safer with us than stuck in either the Russian accounts or Galactix. That means we've effectively left Logan Spencer on the hook for embezzling funds from the Kremlin. But they are funds that the Kremlin can't admit to owning!"

"I think this passes the original objectives of the FSB Mission by putting Spencer on the hook with the Kremlin. But it also provides some self-enrichment. And we've had a successful music tour! All jobs done and in a way that is very difficult to detect. Now we need to get back to Seattle and create a stir there before flying to Washington.

"Why create a stir in Seattle? " Asked Eckhart,

"Alibi, of course! I feel an impromptu gig going on," said Christina,

"I can probably help with that!" said Eckhart.

"You know what, I was going to call Rishi and get us some serious exposure," said Christina.

"He can put the word out on social media and whip us up a crowd! Let me ask him about venues!"

Christina called Rishi. She could tell that he was excited. She placed the phone on the table. "Rishi, I'm on speaker."

"You should think about something at the Seattle Centre" he said, "It is so central and a well known venue. If you really want to blow their minds then I suggest the EMP Sky Church. It's only a small capacity - around 800, I think but is has the most amazing lights and LED screens. If you had Press along and the mallets, it would be awesome. My friend Katsura Makiko works there. I haven't seen her for years but I know she says it is a banging venue."

"Okay Rishi. How would you like to help us with this gig? Fly over to Seattle, spend time with your buddy - light and sound prep us a show? All expenses paid by us?"

Silence.

"Did you just asked me to come to Seattle to sound and vision-scape Christina Nott? All expenses paid?"

"Oh, and your time paid, of course," said Christina.

"I can't say No, I'd be honoured, I really don't know what to say!"

"Yes would be good and, Rishi, bring mallets!"

Christina looked at Eckhart and Chuck, "Look I know that seemed extravagant, but this way we can be certain of a show that will hit the newspapers and mainstream media. I love the idea of an 800-seater venue and then to create demand for plenty more."

Eckhart nodded, "this is going to be some gig!"

"And some alibi!" added Chuck.

"We'd better ring the others now and tell them what is happening."

"I texted Irina to say everything was done, but I have not told her how much we made yet," said Eckhart.

"I think that is better face-to-face. I'll do the same with Clare, although I think she'll have heard via the boys in London."

As if on cue, Christina received a row of smiley faces on her iPhone from Clare.

"Yep, Clare knows."

"Well delightful as it is, sitting here in Lower Manhattan, I think we need to make our way back to JFK. Tell me you have both packed?" asked Chuck.

"Yes, bag is checked into the luggage at the hotel," said Christina. They both looked at Eckhart, "Oh yes, me too."

"Okay, let's get a car from here that can take us back to the hotel, load up and then to JFK," said Chuck.

Chuck was already walking toward several black Town Cars parked at the junction of Fulton and South Street, adjacent to Pier 17.

EMP

*The EMP pulse can easily span continent-sized areas,
and can affect systems on land, sea, and air.*

*The signal from such an event extends
to the visual horizon as seen from the burst point.*

EMP Commission Critical National Infrastructures Report

Back in Seattle

"Here we are, back in the tranquil lands," said Christina.

They didn't need to visit the belts for luggage, because all three of them had managed with just hand luggage in New York.

"I'm amazed you managed to pack that suit!" said Chuck.

"It's all in the fold," said Christina.

They walked outside towards the cab ranks and then suddenly saw Clare, Ellie and Jallie T jumping up and down.

"We decided to come and meet you, Rishi is already here!" said Clare, "He was very excited,"

"Wow, he must have jumped onto a plane almost as soon as I finished speaking to him," said Christina. "We took our time; we should have looked at the timetables first, ah well."

They made their way back to the Fairmont and paused in the Lobby.

"I wonder if I'll get the same room?" asked Christina, "It is starting to get difficult to remember room numbers."

"I remember travelling once on a long US trip. We stayed at Marriotts everywhere. It was also difficult to remember whether it was a left-hand or a right-hand room."

"I know that one," said Christina, "Like the chain with the erratic booking system where you'd sometimes walk into someone else's room."

"Yep - done that too," said Chuck.

Christina took Clare to one side to explain how New York had gone and that they were running the extra gig to create an alibi.

They could see Eckhardt explaining to Irina, and a shocked look on her face.

Irina walked over to Christina, "Look, forgive me for asking, but we will see our money, won't we?"

Christina hugged Irina, " Of course you will, silly, we were simply moving it out of harm's way. I don't think you and Eckhart had thought through the best way to handle such a lot."

"Tomorrow Chuck and I will give you a crash course in money management, which I think is something entirely new for both of you."

There was a hubbub at the main entrance and the other members of Jallie T's band walked in.

"Rishi!" called Christina, seeing that Rishi was with Lucas and the band."

"Hey," he said, smiling and bounded over. "Can I introduce too to my friend Katsura Makiko? She is the one that originally put me on to the EMP Sky Church!"

"Kat, call me Kat," she said, with a slight bow, " I have just been hearing your songs, sung by Alex, sorry Jallie T here - they are terrific. And in the EMP they are quite cosmic."

"We tried out a couple of other Nirvana songs too, said Alex, "As Teen Spirit went down so well in the Arena."

"The tickets all sold out in about ten minutes," said Rishi. We put a rumour on a couple of fan sites and boom. The Sky Church said it was a first. And oh - Thank you so much for bringing me over for this. I'm honoured to be designing the show's lights! Lucas has been working on the sound too. I think you'll like it."

"Okay, you're going to hate me for this, but I think I'd better take a look at the venue," said Christina.

Jallie T put her hand in the air and made a circle, like "One more time now," and the band whooped and then obediently followed her back to the outside of the hotel. The bus was still there, and they filed into it.

EMP Sky Church

They watched as the bus threaded through the traffic, finally arriving at a venue close to the Space Needle.

"It's amazing!" said Christina, looking at the collection of buildings forming the EMP museum, "It looks like so much tin foil has been wrapped around the structures!

"Frank Gehry designed the building. It celebrates all of pop music. Paul Allen ex-Microsoft put up the money for it and it features an extensive Jimi Hendrix collection inside - hence the name Experience Music Project."

"Oh, I thought it stood for Electro Magnetic Pulse?" said Chuck, "Like an EMP wave?"

"It is probably a knowing play on words," said Christina, "But look at this venue!" It's brilliant! You can do things in here that just wouldn't work on those arena stages!"

"Oh trust me, I've got just about every gizmo built into the show!" said Rishi. You can use more or less the same moves as the other evening, but the lighting and backdrop will be 10 times more intense!"

Play On, Christina Nott

Ellie was strumming a bass like. Nate caught it on the guitar and Jallie T stated singing.

With the lights out, it's less dangerous
  Here we are now, entertain us
  I feel stupid and contagious
  Here we are now, entertain us

Wow! Said Christina, "You guys are so together now,"

Raff beat a short tattoo on the drums, and they changed into Feel Your Body all over Mine, one of Christina's songs. Then Hey DJ.

Christina had started singing in Feel Your Body all over Mine and sang the whole of Hey DJ with Jallie T providing the chorus for Hey DJ.

"Nice," said Alex.

"Mind blowing," said Christina looking at the back projection and lights.

"We can send you some flames and drops if you like said Richi over the house speakers.

"Save it for the show, and then surprise me!" said Christina.

"What, like this?" said Rishi as he fired a quick bast of laser light across the stage. It spelled Christina Nott.

"Wow." Said Christina, we can have some fun with this show!"

Ed Adams

The Manhattanite - Music News

Christina Nott was in the House.

Christina Nott has been on world tour, usually with another act Erebus, but tonight for the privileged few, alone playing a not-so-intimate gig to a mere crowd of 800 fans.

This is one group of well-qualified musicians. We, the Press, were even lucky to get tickets to this Wednesday's show at the EMP Sky Church.

Christina Nott is mostly known in Europe as a solo performer, but in an inspired moment has joined up with Jallie T and her band to form the Christina Nott Band for these shows.

They rocked their way through all 14 of Christina Nott's original singles as well as some extra tracks 'just for Seattle'.

This started from the very beginning of the concert, when Nate played the chorus from Nirvana's Teen Spirit which then segued into Nott's Hey DJ.

Play On, Christina Nott

Someone had set the light show to stun as well. There were blasters firing light into the crowd and the huge back wall at the EMP ran several Christina Nott videos as well as live coverage from the concert.

This hardened music critic was dazzled beyond all expectations. If I'd been at Dylan goes electric, Hendrix burns a guitar or the Pistols play the 100 Club, I doubt whether I could have been any more impressed. This was contemporary music makes a seismic shift.

In fact, we wondered about the real Puget earthquakes last night, low on the scale, but whether Christina Nott had programmed them into her set.

They say that sport Arenas record high decibels from big games. 137 decibels seems to be around the limit. When the band started Smells like Teen Spirit again for the second time, we were hoping for a repeat of what happened at their stadium gig earlier in the week.

By all accounts this was better! Christina Nott, Jallie T and Ellie the bassist all swapped into Seattle Seahawks blue tops and brought out pink pom-poms. The noise level was electrifying. The EMP was sending waves out across the Pacific.

I haven't mentioned the crazy little hammers yet. Heart shaped hammer heads on little mallets. Shocking pink illuminations with fans beating them in time with the music.

Then, around two thirds of the way into the set, further mayhem. It looked like a stage invasion by some of the fans.

Security wasn't used to this kind of thing at a venue maybe better known for respectable legends.

Christina and Jallie T shouted 'Crash' to the band and they went into a slow number. Then Christina and Jallie T did hip-hop verses over it. Whilst they did it, Christina, Jallie and Ellie used their pom-poms to gently and good-naturedly shoo the invaders off the stage.

Christina: Not saying its the company you keep
   Not saying its your moods
   Not say-in' its the way you spike your hair
   But some of ya
   Some of ya
   Some of ya stuff ain't normal

Jallie T: Not sayin' its the vodka in the fridge
   ' those bottles full a' broken glass
   Not sayin' its the way you shake your skin
   But some of ya
   Some of ya
   Some of ya stuff aint normal

Christina: I c-can't understand it
   I can't take a lead
   Those chains and studs are cool
   You gotta a certain attitude whenever
   I raise these things
   but some of your stuff ain't normal

Together: I'm sayin'
   Some of your stuff ain't normal
   Yeah some of your stuff
   Ain't normal.

Play On, Christina Nott

Well. After that, what could they do?

Christina came forward and said -'This one's for the FANS' and then they played their way through another anthem. I'd guess they were competing with 136 decibels of crowd by this time. Hooray for Bilsom ear protectors.

Oh yes, and part way through this they let the lasers rip, and of course, the smoke machines.

Whoever was working the control tower was certainly having fun.

And you know what? This hardened music critic was having fun. My best night out in an age. By Far.

BBC America News

Extraordinary fan-footage tonight as the British act Christina Nott played in concert in Seattle. Nott perfumed there a few days ago and this was a smaller intimate session for a few fans.

The venue, Seattle's EMP Sky Church was packed with a sold-out capacity crowd of 800, and there were reportedly more than a thousand fans outside of the venue, causing hastily erected LCD screens to be used for the excess fans to enjoy a free show.

A phenomenon of the Christina Nott supporter is the pink mallets they carry and which they beat rhythmically in time with the songs, in a manner akin to earlier acts highlighted with cigarette lighters or mobile phone torches.

The stage invasion part way through the show showed just how much control the band had of the fans, getting them to leave the stage quietly and then playing the reward of a special song 'This one's for the FANS'.

Fairmont, breakfast buffet.

Christina was having breakfast with Rishi in the Fairmont, before he headed back to Tokyo.

They spotted Irina and Eckhart and Christina held up a newspaper - which had syndicated copy from the Manhattenite. The BBC America channel was playing the same news in the background.

"Mission accomplished, " she said to Irina and Eckhart.

Triples all round

Setup Spencer

Christina said a long goodbye to Rishi and then Irina, Eckhart and Christina were together to discuss the next stage of the sting on Spencer.

"Okay, so Spencer thinks he has got everything set up now, for him to agree with Saito Eiji and broker the deal with Chuck Desjardins," said Eckhart.

"Spencer is usually based on the East Coast, Miami, New York, Atlantic City and Washington D.C. Which is why we have suggested our meeting in one of those places," said Irina.

"Now this is where we need to use some proper FSB leverage," said Christina, "For Shrike to see that your mission has worked it will need someone heavy duty from the Kremlin to attend the next meeting with Spencer.

Christina mused, "It is also interesting, because only now do I realise that the money in play needed to be large. Spencer would have a way to 'find' $200 million if he needed to pay off a debt. But when it is $1.2 billion, that is another story.

Irina said, "We should call Shrike and ask what to do. We must ensure that Shrike thinks that Spencer is holding on to the money though, in other words, he has used his Galactix company to steal the money from the other Russian laundering accounts."

Iriana put through a call to Shrike and after it had gone through the various protocol bumps, she was finally connected.

"Hello, and how is your mission running?" asked Shrike.

Irina started to tell the story, "It has worked well. Logan Spencer thinks he is getting a free loan of $180 million in return for putting his name on a new tower block in Minato City, Tokyo.

"We called in a favour with the Inagawa-kai and Saito Eiji-san persuaded Logan Spencer and Kayden Lowe that he needed the Spencer name for a new Tower Block."

Eckhart added, "Then he met some Russian backers who dropped out of the deal because Logan had double-crossed one of the in the past. We had Pavle Darchidze in that meeting for further authenticity."

"So you put Spencer on a roller-coaster?" said Shrike.

"Yes," said Irina, "Logan was forced to go to the US-billionaire owner of space exploration company Galactix, who wanted a tower block in Minato City, to impress Japan that he was serious about working with them on the JAXA - Japan Aerospace Exploration Agency - project.

Irina added, "This is where things go wrong for Spencer. He thinks he has done a deal with Galactix, but what he has actually done is transferred money from an FSB-owned set of companies into Galactix. He shows up as the Director owner of Galactix."

"I see," said Shrike, "So you have ensured Spencer needs the money from the American, as a further backer for the Project?"

Eckhart started to explain, "At this point Spencer owes the Kremlin all of the money he has transferred into Galactix. But it has gone. He has nothing to repay the Kremlin."

Shrike interrupted,"But where has the money gone? And how much was there?"

"That is the beauty of the scheme. There was no money, but Spencer thinks that there was $1.2 billion. That is the amount we need the FSB to quote when they ask for it back. It is too much for even Spencer to magic from somewhere else."

"I see, so we have Spencer cornered, a strong case of kompromat."

"Exactly," said Irina.

"This has been good work," said Shrike. Now where are you planning for the next meeting with Logan Spencer?"

"We had originally planned it to be in Washington, but he has too many of his acolytes around him there. We thought we should move it to his home-from-home in Miami. It seems very fitting that he would be approached there, on the doorstep of the Russian Mafia. He flies down to Miami most weekends and takes a circus of other people along with him. They have to pander to his ego and in return he introduces them to one other and to ways that they can all get on in business."

Shrike considered for a moment, "Okay, I think I will bring in the heavy guns for this meeting. We can probably get Streltsov Foma Ruslanovich to come along."

"Ruslanovich? He is one scary individual," observed Irina," Are you sure?"

Shrike continued, "Foma Ruslanovich has developed his own dark network within the Russian prosecutor's office. He is well versed with the ways of *kompromat*. The prosecutor's office is a den of vipers, and people like Ruslanovich jostle for position by collecting kompromat."

There was a pause. It sounded as if Shrike was sipping a drink, then he continued "Ruslanovich had an ally, Miljan Volny, who was the head of the prosecutor's property department, a sort of miniature version of the Kremlin's Property Department.

That's how Ruslanovich rose to power. By using the taped kompromat from Volny based on a planned uprising.

"Volny wired most of the apartments he handed out. He got a video tape of a politician *in flagrante delicto,* telling a couple of honey-trap women about a plan to overthrow the leadership."

"You see what I meant about Saint Petersburg still being wired?" said Irina to Christina.

Christina said, "So - we're sending a nasty person to rattle Spencer's cage."

"Oh yes," said Eckhart, "Nasty and feared,"

"So where for the meeting?" asked Christina.

"We have thought of somewhere special, " said Eckhart, "Somewhere to appeal to Spencers's ego. It's at the SkyLounge of the 1000 Museum Tower."

"Sounds cool, " said Christina, " I take it we are on an upper floor?"

"Oh yes," said Eckhart, "It is at the very top of the 1000 Museum, which was designed by Zaha Hadid, who some refer to as a starchitect. She was described as 'the queen of the curve' for some of her stellar buildings. And the only thing above the lounge is...a helipad. It is bound to appeal to Spencer's ego, flying into the tallest building in Miami for a power-meeting."

"Except he will leave with a bad taste in his mouth!" said Christina.

"But maybe with a few ideas for buildings that are not just boxes sprayed gold," agreed Eckhart.

Miami 1000 Tower

Three days later and Logan Spencer had been able to move his calendar to accommodate the next meeting with the Minato City Tower Project. He was due to fly in for the mid-morning meeting.

"He'll be late," said Eckhart, "So far he has been late for every meeting. It is part of his way of working. Show the others who the boss is!"

Eckhart, Irina and Christina sat around the table. Eckhart was looking sightly jet-lagged with the continual zig-zagging around the United States.

Ruslanovich had said he would wait outside until Spencer had arrived, so that he could be seen to be the late arrival. It would stir things up with Spencer.

Ruslanovich had also brought Miljan Volny, who could talk with some authority about bugging buildings. They were going to accuse Spence of wiring other buildings he had contracted in New York, Washington and Miami. All it required was for Volny to disclose his techniques and show some grainy footage of a diplomat in a compromising situation. The tapes they had brought had been modified to show Spencer Building identities instead of Volny's own apartments.

It was time for the meeting and they sat drinking iced water. "This is becoming a habit," said Christina. The others nodded. "Lets take bets," suggested Eckhart, "About how late he will be. I say 30 minutes."

"I wonder who he will bring this time? He seems to get through lawyers at an alarming rate."

"I expect they all quit when he refuses to pay them, " said Eckhart. Christina and Irina laughed.

The room for the meeting had been wired so that Ruslanovich could hear. He sat in another room with Volny. Everyone had decided it was too risky to include Chuck and they needed the deniability of the US Billionaire, for the rest of the Spencer story to stick. This could be Spencer and maybe Kaydon Lowe's word against Irina, Eckhart and Christina.

They could hear a slight noise from outside. They were aware that a helicopter had landed upon the roof.

"He got his helicopter specially registered in Georgia, the country, you know. It's 4LO-GAN, said Irina.

They laughed. They could hear noise outside of the room. In came a familiar security person, then second one and then Logan Spencer, Kayden Lowe and a lawyer. It was a new different lawyer.

"Good afternoon, Mr Spencer," began Irina.

He looked at the people in the room but didn't seem to recognise any of them.

"So where is Saito Eiji?" asked Spencer.

"His representative will be along in a minute," answered Irina.

On cue, a helicopter flew past the window of the SkyLounge.

"I think that will be him now," said Irina.

A second helicopter flew past and then a third.

"I think Eiji-san's representative travels with security," said Irina, "Those two outrider helicopters are both gunships, made to look like regular commercial flights."

Spencer was being outplayed.

Ruslanovich was already in the building, the helicopters were purely for show.

"Please take a seat and help yourself to the refreshments, we also have ice cold Coca-Cola and water."

Spencer sat and then so did Lowe and the lawyer. Spencer had still not asked for introductions nor introduced the lawyer.

Irina introduced each of them, and then it came to the lawyer's turn.

"Raanan Rothstein, from Shackelov and Partners LLP, he explained.

Christina could vaguely remember something about the Shackelov firm specialising in non-profits and yet somehow the partners getting a massive payoff. It had been a scandal for a couple of weeks and tied back to several well-known people.

Christina remembered Irina's advice to assume that everyone would be a crook of some kind, whilst she wondered how Spencer was working with a non-profit lawyer.

There was a further noise at the door and two dark-suited wired up heavies entered. They were from FSB Central Casting. Then Ruslanovich and Volny entered the room, and then a further three men, whom Christina assumed to be lawyers. The last man was also carrying a DSLR camera.

"Hello, Mr Spencer, My name is Streltsov Foma Ruslanovich and this is my close associate Miljan Volny. You seem to have been very busy with some of our assets."

Logan started to introduce Kayden Lowe and Raanan Rothstein.

"Mr Spencer," interrupted Ruslanovich, "I know who these people are, I also know who you used as lawyers for the last two meetings associated with this project. You are careless with lawyers, Mr Spencer, just as you seem careless with other people's money."

Logan was not used to someone so quickly gaining the upper hand in a meeting.

"Well, if you feel like this about things then I'll walk away from the deal," said Spencer trying to use a nuclear option to change direction.

Ruslanovich laughed, "You walk away. That is rich. You come to my associate Mr Saiti Eiji and he kindly offers you much money for your branding. It was a great offer. But you decide to take matters into your own hands. To steal from us. You may not know it, but you were stealing from the Kremlin when you took that money into Galactix."

"But I didn't," said Spencer, "Galactix was providing me with money, from its Russian subsidiaries. Galactix was to pay me the rest of the investment money related to the Tokyo deal."

"Come, come Mr Spencer, You are being economical with the truth. You took the money and placed it into your Space Exploration company. I can see how it made sense to take money from five Russian companies making Space exploration components, but did you really think you would get away with that?"

"I don't know what you are talking about," blustered Spencer.

Kayden chipped in, "I was at the meetings, we simply took the money on behalf of the investors in Spencer Tower in Tokyo."

"Took is your word. I prefer stole," said Ruslanovich.

"We want the money back," said Volny, " I have checked the amount transferred to your Galactix company. It was $1.144 billion. On daily compounded interest, it is already 1.18 billion."

"But that is impossible," said Spencer. The amount I agreed with Desjardins was only $650 million."

"Ah, so you are not denying that you requested money then?" asked Volny.

Christina could see that Ruslanovich could easily play the bad guy but was giving the role to Volny. Instead of Good Guy/Bad Guy it would be Bad Guy/Terrifying Guy.

Volny said, "Look, I don't care how you got into this situation, but right now you'll need to put it right. Pay us back or we'll take other sanctions Mr Spencer."

Spencer looked over to Kayden Lowe and to his lawyer.

Raanan Rothstein state to reply, "You are being particularly harsh on Mr Spencer, he will contest this claim of yours and it appears to represent extortion with menaces."

"Stop!" said Ruslanovich," You think you can use your bent lawyer to represent you. The one that has stolen money from many low-income innocent people whilst pretending to be a Christian Charity. And then paying himself and his partners huge bonuses. We have the material on that.

"You can say goodbye to your Shakelov firm, pretending to be all Russian Jewish. It's disgraceful. Mr Rothstein, be ready to get you own Wikipedia entry as the man who brought down the Shackelov Partners LLP."

"Okay," said Spencer, "What do you want?"

"We are grown adults here. You understand the meaning of kompromat? I think we have plenty on you now. 1.2 billion items and increasing daily. We'll want you to work with us. You know what as a special offer I will include

Mr Rothstein and Kayden Lowe too. There, three for the price of one. You will need to do as we say. You will become agents for the FSB. Don't worry, we won't send you running up walls like Mr James Bond. No, you will be able to walk into the powerful rooms, through the doors, and bring us some things back.

"We own you, Mr Spencer. Oh, and your colleagues, here."

"But what about my security detail?"

"Oh we have owned them for a long time? *Dobrogo dnya, mal'chiki*!"

"*Privet Boss, kak dela*?" Spencer's security detail variously answered Ruslanovich in Russian. "Hi Boss, How are you?"

"But Spencer, this is not all bad news for you. We will be helping you reach greater office in the US Administration. Maybe the top office. You simply need to continue as you are doing. Who knows, we may give you a helping hand with some of those failing projects of yours.

"In return, you'll keep allowing us to launder money and we will promote you to the greatest positions of power, from where you can serve the Kremlin."

"Make no mistake though, try to double cross us and your whole family line will be eliminated, probably after we have torn down your reputation. Show him the tape, Miljan.

Volny plugged a laptop into the room projector. Some grainy footage appeared - it showed an American senator talking to a woman, maybe his wife. He was criticising the government.

Then it cut to another scene. Two men talking, a different room, the skyline looked like New York. This time it was a racism conversation. Not attractive.

"Enough," said Ruslanovich, "These are a couple of examples from the apartments you have built all over New York, Washington and here in Miami. We have hundreds more. Proof that you have wired the apartments and monitor the high-profile guests."

Ruslanovich and Volny looked at Spencer. To Christina's surprise he didn't start to deny it.

"I don't know where you got this, but you leave me no choice, I accept your deal. You help me out, get me promoted and I'll work for you, undercover of course. Kayden and Rothstein will also co-operate to avoid your threats."

Christina was surprised to see Logan Spencer fold so easily. The offer of further propulsion of his career must have been too good for him. Low ethics and high ego. And now he was in the FSB's pocket.

Seattle Fairmont

The band plus Clare had stayed in Seattle, awaiting the return of Christina. After all, it was only a short hop back to Vancouver. Erebus had stayed on too, although there were clear rifts in the band now. Darius had created them, by his blend of embezzlement and then sharing of band secrets. The Seattle gig was being talked about in social media as 'The Erebus Farewell Gig'

An interview with a music paper revealed what the band thought. It was Marco that said it.

'We should have thought carefully when we named the band after the dark region of Hades in Greek mythology. We have certainly become the Gods of Darkness. Maybe that is the name for our next album.

"Will that be your farewell album too?" Asked the interviewer.

Christina, Eckhart, Irina and Chuck arrived back at the hotel.

"Hey!" said everyone, " I think this is the end of the tour!"

"I know, things kind of swooped away from us at the end," said Christina," And you know what, I decided that you've been such a great band and created so much positive publicity, that I want to give you all a bonus. I've arranged it with Clare and she is going to bank transfer you a sum that can be divided six ways - that's to include Lucas, of course."

Alex spoke, "That's really not necessary, because we have had an absolute blast! Tell us if you want to do another tour and give us first refusal!"

"...But on the other hand, we are always glad of the money!" added Nate laughing.

"Don't worry, it should see you all do fine," said Christina.

Clare nodded, "I'll get on to it, and I might just slip a small part of the Triangle money that way as well," she said winking towards Christina.

"And as for this trendy billionaire," said Alex, looking towards Chuck, who was still in new clothes bought on Rodeo Drive, "We'd hardly know him from the dusty cowboy that walked in at the beginning of the tour."

Christina looked towards Eckhart and Irina, "I got something for us all when we were in Saint Petersburg," she said.

"It was after one of our chats in the hotel. I went to the shop. I've been carrying these around ever since."

She fished into her bag and produced three tiny sacks, the kind that jewellery is carried in.

"Here," she said,

"One for each of us! It seems appropriate now that we've finished each of the three missions."

- Music - check.
- Manipulation - check.
- Money - check.

Irina and Eckhart looked into the small bags.

"Perfect!" said Irina, and hugged Christina,

"Yes - Perfect," said Eckhart.

They laid the three silver Russian coins of Peter the Great next to one another.

"Here's to Saint Petersburg," said Christina.

www.ingramcontent.com/pod-product-compliance
Lightning Source LLC
Chambersburg PA
CBHW071725080526
44588CB00013B/1896